REGGAE

Deep Roots Music

by

Howard Johnson

and

Jim Pines

PROTEUS BOOKS
LONDON and NEW YORK
In association with
CHANNEL FOUR TELEVISION

PROTEUS BOOKS is an imprint of
The Proteus Publishing Group

United States
PROTEUS PUBLISHING COMPANY, INC.
9 West 57th Street, Suite 4503
New York, NY 10019
distributed by:
CHERRY LANE BOOKS COMPANY, INC.
P.O. Box 430
Port Chester, NY 10573

United Kingdom
PROTEUS BOOKS LIMITED
Bremar House, Sale Place
London W2 1PT
distributed by:
J. M. DENT & SONS (DISTRIBUTION) LIMITED,
Dunhams Lane, Letchworth
Herts. SG6 1LF

ISBN 0 86276 117 4 (paperback)
ISBN 0 86276 119 0 (hardback)

First published in U.S. 1982
First published in U.K. 1982

Copyright © 1982 Howard Johnson and Jim Pines

All rights reserved. No part of this book may be
reproduced in any form or by any electronic or
mechanical means including information storage and
retrieval systems without permission in writing from
the Publisher, except by a reviewer who may quote
brief passages in a review.

Editor Chris Goodwin
Designed by Sharmans
Typeset by Wordsmiths,
West End, Street, Somerset
Printed and Bound in Great Britain by
Blantyre Printing & Binding Co., Glasgow

REGGAE
Deep Roots Music

A Cultural History of Jamaican Popular Music

Interviews, Research & Text by
Howard Johnson & Jim Pines
Photographs by **Howard Johnson**

Acknowledgements

Sylvia Mingay who was the first person to read the manuscript and give it a boost; Deborah London for all the help she gave; Jeremy Isaacs for having the vision to commission the series "Deep Roots Music"; Chris Goodwin of Proteus for being so patient and encouraging; Susannah Jaeger for putting the deal together; Mike Wallington for his encouragement; David Rodigan for his help and information over the years; Chris Pring for the brilliant design of this book.

Photographs courtesy of:
    Royal Commonwealth Society
    Afro-Caribbean Institute
    National Library of Jamaica

Research material courtesy of:
    Jamaica Journal
    Institute of Jamaica

This book is dedicated to the Jamaican people, Pepe Judah; Willie who took me to my first sound system dance to hear the great Duke Reid in 1955; David Mingay editor of the series **Deep Roots Music**; Joseph Papp who taught me about musicals; and to Julian-Ali Johnson who I hope will read this book one day.

Howard Johnson

(Producer and Director
Deep Roots Music)

CONTENTS

	FOREWORD	vii
	Eulogy to Black Artists	viii
I	**AFRICAN ROOTS AND REVIVAL**	12

The African Cultural Heritage — Maroon culture: Myal and Kumina — The secular tradition: Jonkonnu and Buru — We need a Revival

II	**FROM MENTO TO REGGAE**	45

Mento — Ska — Rock Steady — Reggae

III	**RANKING SOUNDS**	65

Sound Systems: Duke Reid — The art of Toasting: Count Machouki, Sir Lord Comic, U-Roy, Big Youth

IV	**BLACK ARK, SPIRITUALITY AND REGGAE**	77

The Rastafarian movement: Haile Selassie, Marcus Garvey, beliefs and concepts of Rastafari — Lee 'Scratch' Perry — Jimmy Riley — Dennis Brown — Marcia Griffiths

V	**MONEY IN MY POCKET**	97

Jamaican popular music business in the Sixties — Harry J. (producer) — Neville Lee (distributor) — Problems of commercialisation

VI	**GHETTO RIDDIMS**	111

Jack Ruby — Charlie Ace — Black Kush — Saint John

	Twenty Reggae Albums / Twenty Reggae Singles	124

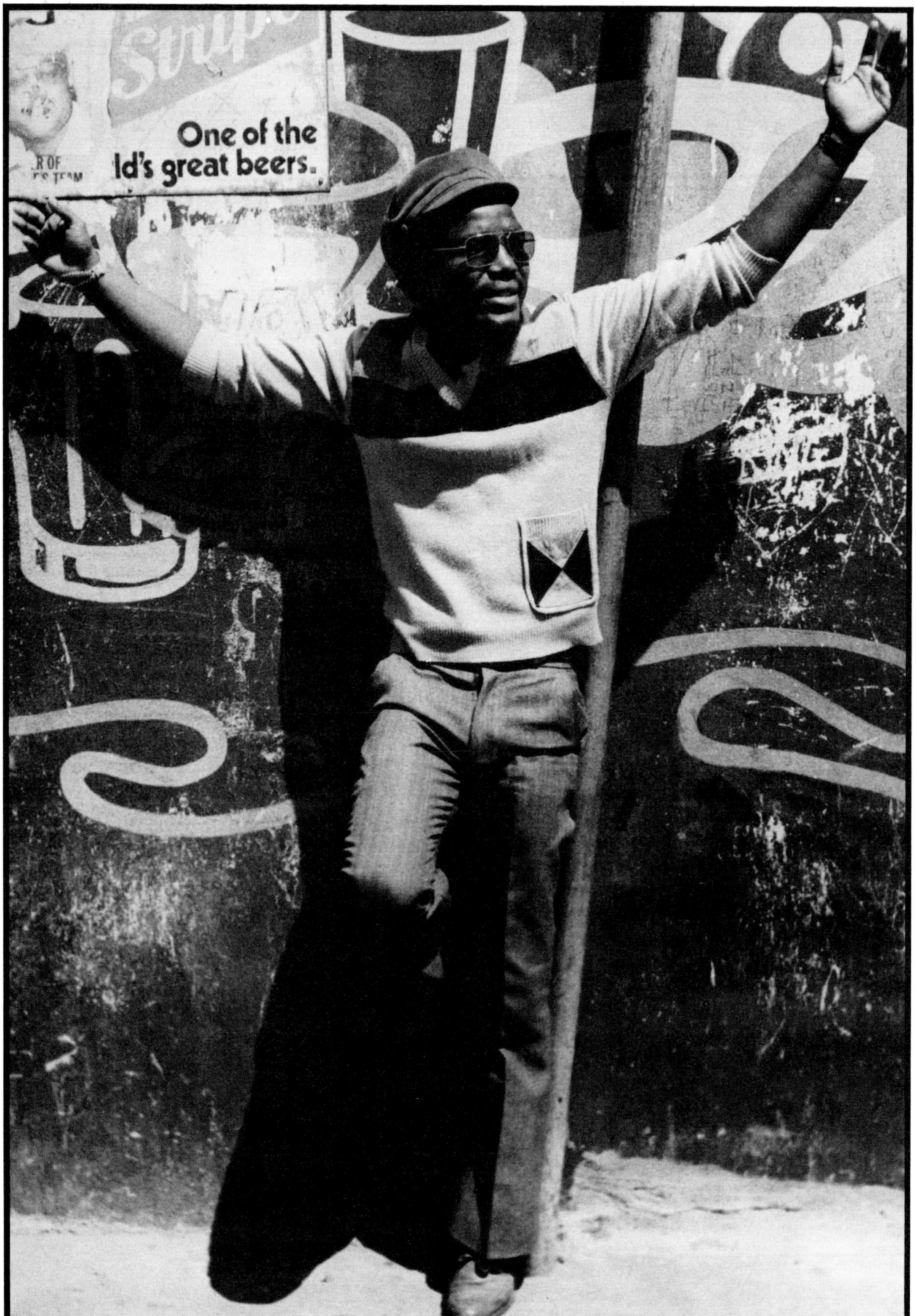
One of the
ld's great beers.

FOREWORD

What other music of international importance has been so plundered, so ignored, without a proper history? Charlie Ace says it: "Reggae music is one of them stones that was refused by the builders."

Reggae is a music of blood, black reared, pain rooted, heart geared. Reggae is a music of fire and brimstone, all tense-up in the bubble and the weight drop. Reggae is a people's music, ghetto people, millions of royal slaves, kidnapped and deported Africans, who stare down Babylon, tear down Bablylon, check the lightening flash, and look to the new Jerusalem. Reggae is the King's music, the jewel in the crown of the Emperor Haile Selassie — I.

Reggae music is all this and more. It is Third World music, struggling music, baldhead music and rasta music, lovers rock and dub. Tributes are paid and played all over the world, in Tokyo, Toronto and Timbuktoo, but the men and women who make the music are Jamaican. Jamaica is the source. It is to this source, to the many springs of Jamaica's music — to folk stories, work songs, African rituals, to swing jazz, mento, R&B and to ska, rock steady and reggae — that this book, and the series of films which accompany it, is dedicated.

Its roots run deep. **Deep** like the balmyard gift of ganja, like the bad bass bounce of 2000-watt boxes, like the ocean that separates I&I from the motherland; **Roots** — the rich dark earth that feeds the avocado seed and gives praises, the ancient talk of buru drums, the rootical new appropriation of the Bible. A **music** of messiahs and messengers, shepherds and obeah-men, latter-day saints and mighty upsetters. Speakers in tongues, and servants of the King.

Deep Roots Music is unique. It goes to places, it listens to people, and it digs around in Jamaica's rich heritage where nobody has been before. It unlocks the lost music of the Maroons and of plantation society, and it traces a line from the buru-men and obeah-men through to today's reggae masters. It shows how Revival and Rastafari have shaped the sound, and why the sound-system became the precious inner sanctum of local black pride. It catalogues the heavy manners that followed the rude-boy and the rasta, and it celebrates the comfort they found in deep roots music.

Like Charlie Ace says it, it is ghetto people who really support this thing: "The stone that the builder refused shall be the head corner stone."

MIKE WALLINGTON
(Executive Producer
Deep Roots Music)

Eulogy to Some of the Great Black Artists

Louis Armstrong, who revolutionised the jazz trumpet, for 'What Did I Do To Be So Black and Blue'; Count Basie, whose flying riffs and rhythms made a huge impact on big band jazz; Blind Blake for 'Search Warrant Blues' and 'Police Dog Blues'; Charles 'Buddy' Bolden, the first great jazz trumpeter and originator of the jazz band; James Brown for 'Please, Please, Please' and 'Get on the Good Foot'; the rootsy blues-jazz artist, Ray Charles, for 'What'd I Say' and 'I Got A Woman'; Nat 'King' Cole, the great jazz pianist and vocalist, for 'Nature Boy'; the genius of John Coltrane, for 'A Love Supreme'; Arthur Crudup for 'Mean Old Frisco' and 'I'm Alright, Mama'; Ornette Coleman, the creator of 'New Jazz'; the great Miles Davis, who has played a major part in every innovation in modern jazz, for 'Kind of Blue' and 'Miles Ahead'; The Reverand Gary Davis for 'You Better Get Right', 'Cocaine Blues'; the brilliant Eric Dolphy for 'Miss Movement' and 'Out to Lunch'; Duke Ellington, for his 5,000 compositions including 'Black and Tan Fantasy' and 'Take the A Train'; Blind Boy Fuller for 'You Got To Have Your Dollar'; The legendary W. C. Handy, Father of the Blues, for 'St. Louis Blues'; the giant tenor saxophonist, Coleman Hawkins, who gave a new voice to the instrument; Fletcher Henderson, the great inspiration behind big band jazz music; the brilliant Jimi Hendrix, creator of the modern rock guitar, for 'Moon Turn The Tides... and Gently Gently Away'; the legendary Lady of the Blues, Billie Holiday, for 'God Bless the Child'; the legendary Son House, Father of the Folk Blues, for 'Preaching Blues' and 'My Black Mama'; Mississippi John Hurt for 'moanin' the Blues'; Milt Jackson for 'Bag's Groove'; Blind Lemon Jefferson for 'Eagle Eyed Mama'; Pete Johnson, whose 'Roll 'Em Pete' (sung by Joe Turner) anticipated the emergence of R & B; the genius of Robert Johnson, the original blues master, for 'Love in Vain Blues', 'Crossroads Blues', 'Terraplane Blues', 'Rambling on My Mind', 'Kindhearted Woman', 'Little Queen of Spades', etc; the brilliant ragtime composer and pianist, Scott Joplin, for 'Maple Leaf Rag'; Rahsan Roland Kirk, the brilliant jazz multi-instrumentalist; the legendary Leadbelly, King of the 12-string guitar; Mance Lepscomb for 'Blues in G'; the brilliant jazz composer, pianist and virtuoso, John Lewis, who shaped the voice of the Modern Jazz Quartet; Fred McDowell for 'Mississippi Delta Blues', 'Some Day Baby' and 'Milk Cow Blues'; the master travelling blues artist Blind Willie McTell, for 'Travelin' Blues' and 'Love Changin' Blues'; Miriam Mikeba, the brilliant vocalist who gave African song a new thrust in the popular idiom; the genius of Charles Mingus, for 'Roots & Blues' and 'What Love'; Memphis Minnie for 'Down House Girl'; Thelonious Monk, the master of the modern jazz piano, for 'Blue Monk'; Little Brother Montgomery for 'Vicksbury Blues'; the legendary Jelly Roll Morton; King Oliver, the great innovator of big band jazz; the genius of Charlie Parker, who opened the way for the development of modern jazz; the jazz virtuoso Oscar Peterson, for 'Hymn to Freedom'; the genuis of Bud Powell, for his 'Hallucinations'; the legendary Gertrude 'Ma' Rainey', Mother of the Blues, for her 'Rough and Tumble Blues'; Smokey Robinson, the great composer of Soul classics; the giant saxophonists Sonny Rollins, for 'St. Thomas'; the legendary Bessie Smith, Empress of the Blues, for 'Poor Man's Blues' and 'Young Woman's Blues'; Art Tatum, who took the jazz piano to its outer limits of expression; Joe Turner, one of the great innovators of early R & B; the great vocalist Sarah Vaughan; Muddy Waters for 'Baby Please Do Go'; Charley

Weaver for 'Two Faced Woman'; the genius of Stevie Wonder for 'Visions' and 'Black Man'; Lester Young, the 'Cézanne of modern jazz', who transformed the voice of the tenor saxophone; Fela Anikulapo Kuti for I.T.T. ('International Thief Thief'); Desmond Dekker for 'Israelites'; the great jazz guitarist Ernest Ranglin for 'Come Back Liza'; Baba Brooks for 'River Bank'; the brilliant trombonist Don Drummond for 'Occupation'; The Ticklers for 'Healing in the Balm Air'; The Jamaican Folksingers for 'Dis Long Time Gal'; the legendary master Rasta drummer Count Ozzie for 'Prepare For the Day'; Georgia St. Thomas Group for 'Throw Me Corn'; Kennedy Bands for 'Maroon Gaun'; Ethiopians for 'Selah'; Carlos Malcolm and the Afro-Jamaicans for 'Nobody's Business'; Frats Quintet for 'Coverly' and 'Come We Go Dung'; Kapo for 'Revival Chorus'; Mancheoneal Group for 'King Power'; and many many more Great Black Men and Women who we haven't mentioned, but whose place in the history of popular music is indelible.

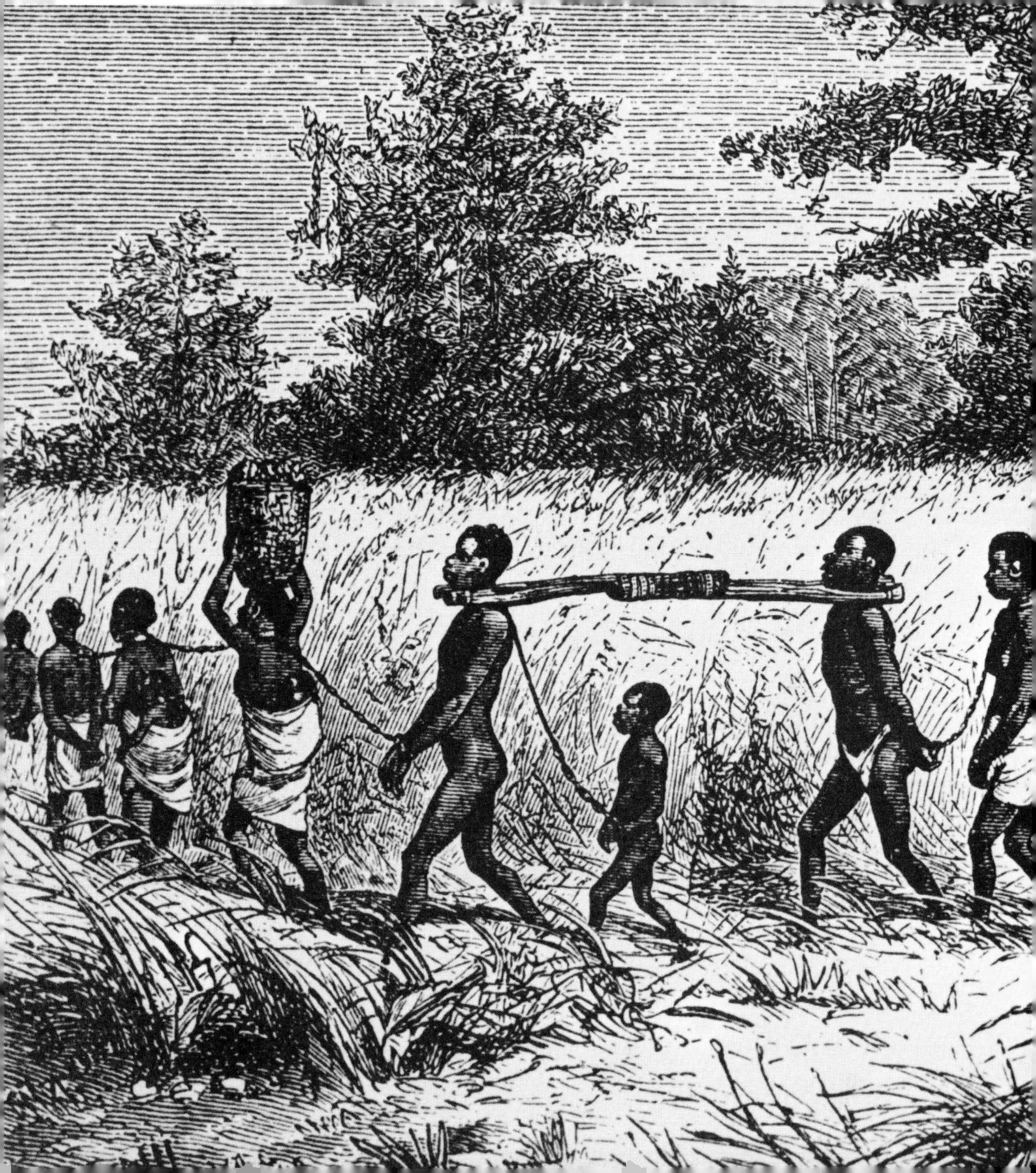

AFRICAN ROOTS AND REVIVAL

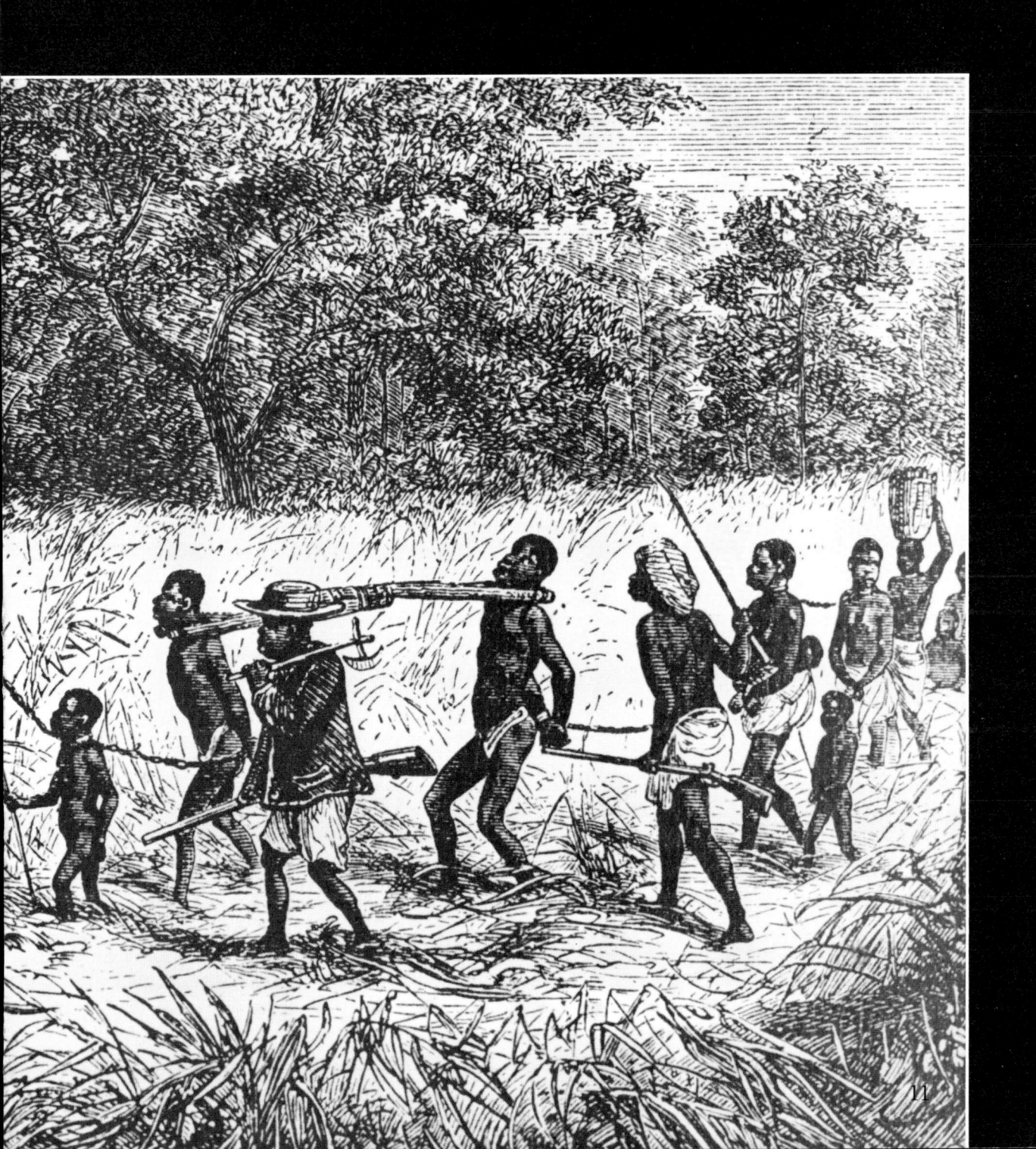

The African Heritage

Many people believe that slavery more or less completely stripped African slaves of their social and cultural heritage. It is often argued that European domination was so powerful that the slaves had no choice but to become part of the dominant (European) culture, or go under. But as the Maroon policy of 'flight or fight' clearly shows, this was not the case. Indeed, there is considerable evidence that African slaves in the New World, even under the brutal plantation system, retained a great deal of their African background. Rather than being culturally absorbed or destroyed by domination, they developed new customs and practices based strongly on their old African traditions.

Jamaica is unique in this respect. The slaves were not encouraged to partake in the white man's culture, so they were left pretty much to themselves to develop their own cultural expressions. This arose because the English Planters were solely concerned with extracting maximum labour from their slaves and were not in the least interested in the slaves' physical or spiritual welfare (except, of course, when it directly affected the economics of the system). They made no attempt to introduce the slaves to European culture or values, and converting 'heathens' to Christianity was out of the question. Jamaica was a kind of factory site, and the imported slaves its machines. Jamaican slavery was an extraordinarily brutal system, one of the worst in the history of slavery.

Left to themselves, the African slaves succeeded against all odds to reconstruct a culture of their own. They were helped by the fact that most of them came from the same coastal area of West Africa and included Ashanti, Fanti, Ibo, Yoruba, Mandingo, and other neighbouring peoples. With their broadly similar backgrounds, and their shared experiences under slavery in the New World, the African slaves found sufficient grounds on which to build a common foundation. Many African cultural themes and images survive today in Western Black culture – for example, place names, names of deities and religious cults (e.g. Jamaican **Kumina**), day names given to newborn children (e.g. Kofi), and so on.

The Africans came from highly organised societies. Indeed, a number of these societies had developed into powerful states, and managed vast empires up to the early 19th century. They included the ancient West African kingdom of Benin (Edo peoples), the Fulani empire and that of the Oyo Yoruba, the Dahomey kingdom and the Ashanti (Akan), to name several of the more famous ones. African societies were essentially agricultural although they had highly developed

An interior view of a Jamaica House of Correction.

systems of trade, markets and labour, as well as a monetary system. This background played no small part in the Jamaican Maroons' own survival in the isolated regions of the island.

Many aspects of African religion were also transplanted to Jamaica, and they continued to play a vital part in the development of Afro-Jamaican culture. In the African tradition, religion is an integral part of daily life, both for the individual and for the community. This tradition, or world view, was strongly maintained by the Maroons and, in a more covert way, by the slaves on the plantations. The Maroons established a form of African religion called **Myal**; this also became the religion of the plantation slaves in the form of **Kumina**.

At the core of Myal/Kumina religion is the African belief that the spirits of the ancestors play an active part in the welfare of the living community. In the African context, this conception is expressed in the form of ancestor worship, and it is closely tied to the maintenance of the kinship group. Rituals are designed to appease the ancestral dead, who are thought to be watching over their descendants and angered if they are neglected. The Africans who were transported to the New World as slaves retained the essential features of this religious conception. Their Myal/Kumina cult groups were the focus of intense religious activity which included invocation and spirit possession; and in sharp contrast to the Judeo-Christian tradition, they adhered to the fundamental African belief in

A Grand Jamaica Ball in Spanish Town.

more than one deity.

Myal/Kumina was expressed in fertility rites, thanksgiving ceremonies, funerals, rites of passage and so on. Ritual occasions such as these were an important source of African cultural identity among the Maroons and the plantation slaves – they had a powerful unifying effect which brought together people from different, though closely related, African cultural backgrounds, and reinforced their sense of solidarity. Myal/Kumina religion thus played a major part in helping the transplanted Africans to survive in their new and brutal condition of slavery.

Like religion, music is an integral part of African society, and has a function in all aspects of culture. There is a wide variety of African musical forms – lullabies, work songs, sacred songs, songs of derision, recreational music, music aimed at celebrating some important event such as harvest, and so on. African music also makes use of an enormous range of instruments – including the ever-present drum (in its many forms), the gong, rattles, flutes, stringed instruments like the 'African harp', the **sanza** or 'African piano', and many others. These instruments are generally used in an accompaniment capacity, rarely on their own. Hence their intimate connection with dance and song. Interestingly, this is reflected in the Jamaican religious and folk tradition, where dance steps have the same names as the musical (or religious) form with which they are associated.

One of the main characteristics of African music is its emphasis on rhythm, particularly polyrhythm. Whereas a piece of European music generally has only one rhythm in operation at any one moment, a piece of African music invariably has two or three, and sometimes even four different rhythms at the same time. African rhythm is closely tied to drumming, although it can equally be seen in hand-clapping, feet-stamping, or in percussive instruments such as the xylophone. One of the drums provides the regular beat and sets the time for the other rhythms and instruments to operate within. With the exception of this drum, the instrumentalists may improvise expansively, provided of course that they keep within the time allowed. African drumming is therefore built up from combinations of rhythmic patterns, and these may include extensive use of off-beats or syncopation.

Another feature of African vocal music is the call-and-response pattern (antiphony), or alternate singing by soloist and chorus. This music device was transplanted intact to the Jamaican cultural setting, and it is one of the principal characteristics of Western black music generally. There has been a long debate in

A Negro hung alive by the ribs to a gallows.

academic circles as to whether African music makes strong use of harmony; this is reflected in the well-known comment that 'Rhythm is to Africa as Harmony is to Europe'. However, there is much harmony in African vocal music, especially within the call-and-response pattern, where there is often overlapping between soloist and chorus in their respective melodic lines. We should add to this the vocal quality, the variety of timbre and use of falsetto and other ornamental devices.

What is clear from these examples is that African music has a complex structure, not just in terms of rhythm (percussion), but also in relation to melody, vocalisation, and so on. This raises the question of the extent to which these elements were transplanted to Jamaica, and whether they were eventually lost through outside (European) influences which the African slaves would have experienced. Pamela O'Gorman, Director of the Jamaican School of Music, suggests, somewhat controversially, that there are significant differences, for example, between African rhythms and contemporary Jamaican rhythms:

'African music is of course much more complicated. You get a great deal more polyrhythm and polymetre in African music than in Jamaican. To our ears – even in Jamaica – African music is exceedingly complex, and in fact it is a music that you have to become attuned to and begin to understand properly. Now, probably one of the main European influences that you find in Jamaican music is the 1-2-3-4/ etc. beat, which you don't find so much in African music. This regular beat in Jamaican music is believed to have come originally from military bands and other European influences that you got in the Caribbean.'

But in other areas, as Pamela O'Gorman

A mill yard.

points out, there are strong similarities between the African and the Jamaican – such as the use of songs of derision, the use of voice (i.e. the same open, relaxed quality), etc. Significantly, she adds: 'In the last ten years or so, we have had African musicologists coming to Jamaica looking for African survivals in our culture. Things that have died out in Africa, they believe, are still alive in Jamaica. For example, among the Maroon community today, you will find a lot of African influences and African speech.' As the following pages set out to show, many of these influences, or survivals, persisted in spite of strong opposition from the status quo. They define the essential character of Afro-Jamaican culture. 'Despite all the pressures and obstacles that were put on Black people, they not only retained a few elements, but managed to keep intact large areas of their culture.' – Garth White, writer and historian of Jamaican culture.

Above – Slave being flogged by another slave while the master looks on. Facing – List of methods of procuring slaves.

R E M A R K S

ON THE

METHODS OF PROCURING SLAVES,

WITH A SHORT ACCOUNT OF THEIR

TREATMENT IN THE WEST-INDIES, &c.

FIG. I.

Represents the manner of Yoking the Slaves by the Mandingoes, or African Slave Merchants, who usually march annually in eight or ten parties, from the River Gambia to Bambouk: each party having from one hundred to one hundred and fifty Slaves.

FIG. III.

Where the roads lay through woods, the captive inhabitants are made to travel several hundred miles with a log hung at heel attached.

FIG. V.

The Husband and Wife, after being sold to different purchasers, violently separated—probably never to see each other more!

FIG. VII.

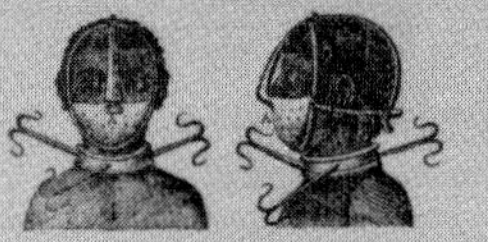

A front and profile view of an African's head with the mouth piece and neck-collar, the hooks round which, are placed as a preventative to an escape when pursued in the woods, or, to preventing of rest by laying the head down.

N.B. At A is a piece of flat iron which goes into the mouth—and so effectually keeps down the tongue, that nothing can be swallowed, not even the saliva, a passage for which is made through holes in the mouth piece.

FIG. IX.

An enlarged view of the mouth piece—which when long worn—becomes so heated as frequently to bring off the skin along with it.

N.B. A late respectable tradesman in London, had an order for a great number of these and other such like instruments—but after they were made, finding the uses they were intended for, he declined sending them.

FIG. XI.

The manner in which some Slaves are placed to be flogged.

THE respectable and increasing numbers of those, who, from motives of Humanity, have concurred in rejecting the produce of West-Indian Slavery, cannot but afford a subject of the sincerest joy to every friend of mankind. Even those who from motives of Interest still favor or engage in the Trade, have been obliged to be silent upon the injustice of first procuring the Negroes, and have not had the hardiness to excuse or palliate the horrors of the MIDDLE PASSAGE: but still they assert that the treatment the Slaves meet with in the West-Indies amply counterbalances their previous sufferings; they have not scrupled to extol a state of servitude as a happy Asylum from African Despotism, and calmly maintain that the condition of the labouring poor in England, is much harder than that of the Negroes in the West-India Islands. Upon this ground the opposers of slavery are willing to meet its advocates, and the design of the following Extracts is to enable the public to form an impartial and decisive judgement upon the subject.

WHEN a Ship arrives at the port in the West-Indies, the Slaves are exposed to sale, (except those who are very ill, they being left in the yard to perish by disease or hunger.) The healthy are disposed of by public auction, the sickly by scramble. The sale by scramble is thus described; the ship being darkened by sails, the purchasers are admitted, who, rushing forward with the ferocity of brutes, seize as many Slaves as they have occasion for. In none of the sales is any care taken to prevent the separation of relatives or friends, but Husbands and Wives, Parents and Children, fig. 5, are parted with as much unconcern as Sheep and Lambs by the Butcher. Abstract of the Evidence page 46 and 47.

With respect to the GENERAL treatment of the Slaves, Mr. Woolrich says, that he never knew the BEST master in the West-Indies use his Slaves so well as the WORST master his servants in England. Abstract of the Evidence see page 53.

To come to a more PARTICULAR description of their treatment it will be proper to divide them into different classes: the first consisting of those bought for the use of the PLANTATION: the second of the IN and OUT-DOOR Slaves.

The Field Slaves are called out by day light to their work; if they are not there in time they are flogged. When put to their work they perform it in rows, and without exception under the whip of Drivers; a certain number of whom are allotted to each gang. Such is the MODE of their labour; as to the TIME of it they begin at Daylight, and continue with two intermissions (one for half an hour in the morning, the other for two hours at noon) till sun set. Besides this they are expected to range about and pick grass for the cattle, either during their two hours REST at noon, or after the fatigues of the day.

SIR G. YONGE adds, that women were in general considered to miscarry from the cruel treatment they met with; and Captain Hall says that he has seen a woman seated to give suck to her Child, roused from that situation by a severe blow from the cart-whip. Abstract of the Evidence see page 53, 54, 55.

THE above account of their labour is confined to that season of the year which is termed OUT OF CROP. In the crop season the labour is of much longer duration. Mr. Dalrymple says, they are obliged to work as long as they can, that is as long as they can keep awake or stand. Sometimes through excess of fatigue they fall asleep, when it has happened to those who feed the Mills, that their arms have been caught therein and torn off. Mr. Cook on the same subject states, that they work in general eighteen hours out of the twenty-four; he knew a Girl lose her hand by the Mill while feeding it, being overcome with sleep she dropped against the rollers. Abstract of the Evidence p. 55, 56.

To this account of their labour, it should be added, that it appears that on some estates the Slaves have Sunday and Saturday afternoon to themselves, on others Sunday only, and on others only Sunday in part. It appears again that IN CROP on no estates have they more than Sunday for the cultivation of their own lands. Abstract of the Evidence page 56.

THE point next to be considered is the FOOD of the Slaves, which appears to be subject to no rule: on some estates they are allowed land, on others provisions, and others are allowed provisions and land jointly. The best allowance is at Barbadoes, of which the following is the account. The Slaves in general, says Gen. Tottenham, appeared to be ill fed; each Slave had one pint of grain for twenty-four hours and sometimes half a rotten Herring. When the Herrings were UNFIT FOR THE WHITES, they were bought up FOR THE SLAVES. Nine pints of corn, and one pound of salt-fish a week, is in general the utmost allowance. As a proof that some have not food enough, Mr. Cook says that he has known both Africans and Creoles eat the putrid carcasses of animals THROUGH WANT. Abstract of the Evidence page 57 and 58.

As to the accusation of their being THIEVES, all the Evidences maintain that it was on account of their being HALF STARVED. Abst. of the Evidence page 58.

CONCERNING the PROPERTY of the field-slaves, all the Evidences agree in asserting that they never heard of a field-slave amassing such a sum as enabled him to purchase his freedom. Abstract of the Evidence page 60.

HAVING now described the state of the plantation, it will be proper to say a few words on that of the IN and OUT-DOOR Slaves.

THE IN-DOOR Slaves are allowed to be better clothed, and fed, and less worked, than the plantation; on account however of being constantly exposed to the cruelty and caprice of their Masters and Mistresses, their lives are rendered so wretched, that they not unfrequently wish to be sent to the field: the OUT-DOOR Slaves are porters, coopers, &c. who are obliged to bring to their Masters a certain sum every day.

THE ordinary punishments of the Slaves are inflicted by the Whip and Cow-skin. This, says Mr. Woolrich, is generally made of plaited Cow-skin, with a thick strong lash, it is so formidable an instrument that some of the overseers can by means of it take the skin off a horse's back, he has seen them lay the marks of it into a deal board: the incisions (according to Dr. Harrison and the Dean of Middleham) are sometimes so deep, that you may lay your finger into the wounds, and are such as no time can erase. As a farther proof of the SEVERITY of the punishments, the following facts are adduced. Mr. Fitzmaurice has known pregnant women so severely whipped as to have miscarried in consequence of it. Davidson knew a Negro Girl die of a mortification of her wounds two days after whipping. Dr. Jackson recollects a Negro dying under the lash or soon after. Abstract of the Evidence see page 66 and 67.

WE now proceed to the EXTRAORDINARY punishments, in the infliction of which, malice, fury, and all the worst passions of the human mind, rage with unbridled licence. Benevolence recoils at the dreadful perspective, and can scarce collect composure to disclose the Bloody Catalogue.

CAPTAIN RAP has known Slaves severely punished, then put into the Stocks, a cattle chain of sixty or seventy pounds weight put on them, and a large collar round their necks, and a weight of fifty-six pounds fastened to the chain, when they were driven afield: the collars are formed with two, three, or four projections, which hinder them from lying down to sleep. See fig. 7 and 8.

A NEGRO man in Jamaica (says Dr. Harrison) was put on the picket so long, as to cause a mortification of his foot and hand, on suspicion of robbing his master, a public officer, of a sum of money, which it afterwards appeared THE MASTER HAD TAKEN HIMSELF. Yet the Master was privy to the punishment and the Slave had no compensation. Abstract of the Evidence page 69.

MR. FITZMAURICE mentions the practice of dropping hot lead upon the Slaves, which he saw performed by a Planter of the name of Rushie in Jamaica, this same man in three years destroyed by severity FORTY NEGROES OUT OF SIXTY. The rest of the conduct of this planter was suppressed by the House of Commons, as containing circumstances TOO HORRIBLE TO BE GIVEN TO THE WORLD.

AN overseer on the Estate where Mr. J. Terry was, in Grenada, threw a Slave INTO THE BOILING CANE JUICE who died in four days.

CAPTAIN COOK relates that he saw a woman named Rachel Lauder, beat a Slave most unmercifully, and would have murdered her had she not been prevented; the girl's crime was, the not bringing money enough from on board of ship, WHITHER SHE HAD BEEN SENT BY HER MISTRESS, FOR THE PURPOSE OF PROSTITUTION.

LIEUTENANT DAVISON relates, that the wife of the Clergyman at Port Royal, used to drop hot sealing wax on her Negroes after flogging—he was sent for as Surgeon to one of them whose breast was terribly burnt.

IF it should be asked for what offences the punishments cited have taken place, the following answer may be given.

UNDER the head of ORDINARY punishments, the Slaves appear to have suffered for not coming to the field in time, not picking a sufficient quantity of grass, for staying too long of an errand, and Theft, to which they were often driven by Hunger.

UNDER the Head of EXTRAORDINARY punishments the following have been alledged as reasons; for running away, for breaking a plate, or to extort confession, in the moments of passion, and one on a diabolical pretence which the master held out to the world to conceal HIS OWN VILLAINY, AND WHICH HE KNEW TO BE FALSE. WOMEN punish their Slaves, for being found pregnant, for not bringing home the FULL WAGES OF PROSTITUTION, and others, without EVEN THE ALLEGATION OF A FAULT.

ALL the facts that have been now adduced are of unquestionable authority, having been extracted from the Evidence laid before the House of Commons by eye-witnesses of the facts. Let now every honest man lay his hand on his breast, and seriously reflect whether he is justifiable in countenancing such barbarities; or whether he ought not to reject with horror, the smallest participation in such infernal transactions. To the weaker sex, whose amicable characteristic it is, to be "tremblingly alive" to every tale of woe, the friends of the Abolition return their warmest acknowledgements, for the zeal with which many of them have espoused the cause of humanity, and for the noble example they have shewn, in rejecting the produce of Slavery and Misery.

FIG. II.

These Log-Yokes are made of the roots of trees—and so heavy as to make it extremely difficult for the person who wears it to walk, much more to escape or run away.

FIG. IV.

A view of the leg bolts or shackles, as put upon the legs of the Slaves on ship board, in the middle passage.

FIG. VI.

When Slaves are purchased by the dealers they are generally marked on the breast with a red hot iron.

FIG. VIII.

A representation of a Slave at work as cruelly accoutered—with a head frame and mouth piece to prevent his eating—with boots and spurs (as they are called) round his legs, and an half hundred weight chained to his body to prevent his absconding.

FIG. X.

An enlarged view of the Boots and Spurs, as seen used on some plantations in Antigua.

FIG. XII.

Another method of tying the poor victims on a ladder to be flogged, which is also occasionally laid flat on the ground for further punishment.

LONDON: PRINTED BY AND FOR DARTON AND HARVEY, No. 55, GRACECHURCH STREET. MDCCXCIV.

[PRICE THREE PENCE.]

Maroon culture: Myal and Kumina

The survival of African elements in Jamaican culture was greatly enhanced by the isolationist character of Maroon society. Having escaped to the mountainous regions of the island, the Maroons established settlements which closely followed the pattern of their lives in Africa. Their economy was agricultural; they retained strong elements of African religion, ritual beliefs and practices, folklore, music and dance, and so on. The introduction of the powerful 'Coromantee' (i.e. mostly peoples of Ashanti origin) beginning in the late 17th century, further strengthened the Maroon cultural base and added a new source of social cohesion (and military expertise) to the ranks of the Maroons.

The Maroons resisted European domination and fought hard to preserve their freedom and independence. Their successful rebellions against slavery and the plantation system enabled them to maintain a considerable degree of autonomy over a fairly long period of time. By cutting themselves off from the influences of Western culture in this way, they were able not only to keep alive their African culture, but to avoid the danger of it being diluted. As a result, Maroon culture became the primary vehicle through which African cultural traditions were maintained and developed in Jamaican society.

Maroon culture and 'plantation culture', however, were not absolutely opposed to each other. In fact, they were closely interconnected in a number of important areas of social life. But they did differ in terms of the intensity with which they were able to articulate African expressions. Maroon culture was far more explicit and radical in its African orientations than was plantation culture, where the African cultural voice was 'modulated' under the weight of plantation ideology. Consequently, it was the Maroons who came to symbolise the 'alternative', militant force within the wider Afro-Jamaican setting. And as such, they were a source of cultural identification for many of the African slaves on the plantations, a number of whom managed to escape to join Maroon communities.

Above – The Maroons in ambush on the Dromilly Estate, Trelawny. Facing – A Coromantyn Free Negro or Ranger, armed.

The Maroons preserved an element of African religion in the form of **Myal**. This was essentially a ritual ceremony concerned with 'spiritual and physical healing', in which spirit possession and the use of herbs featured strongly. The proceedings centred on the magical powers of the cult leader, who was generally known for his exorcism. The Maroons are still noted for their 'Myal men' or 'Myal healers', who continue to conduct such 'healing' ceremonies in Jamaica.

Myal leaders would often use their secret knowledge of herbal 'medicine' (also known as

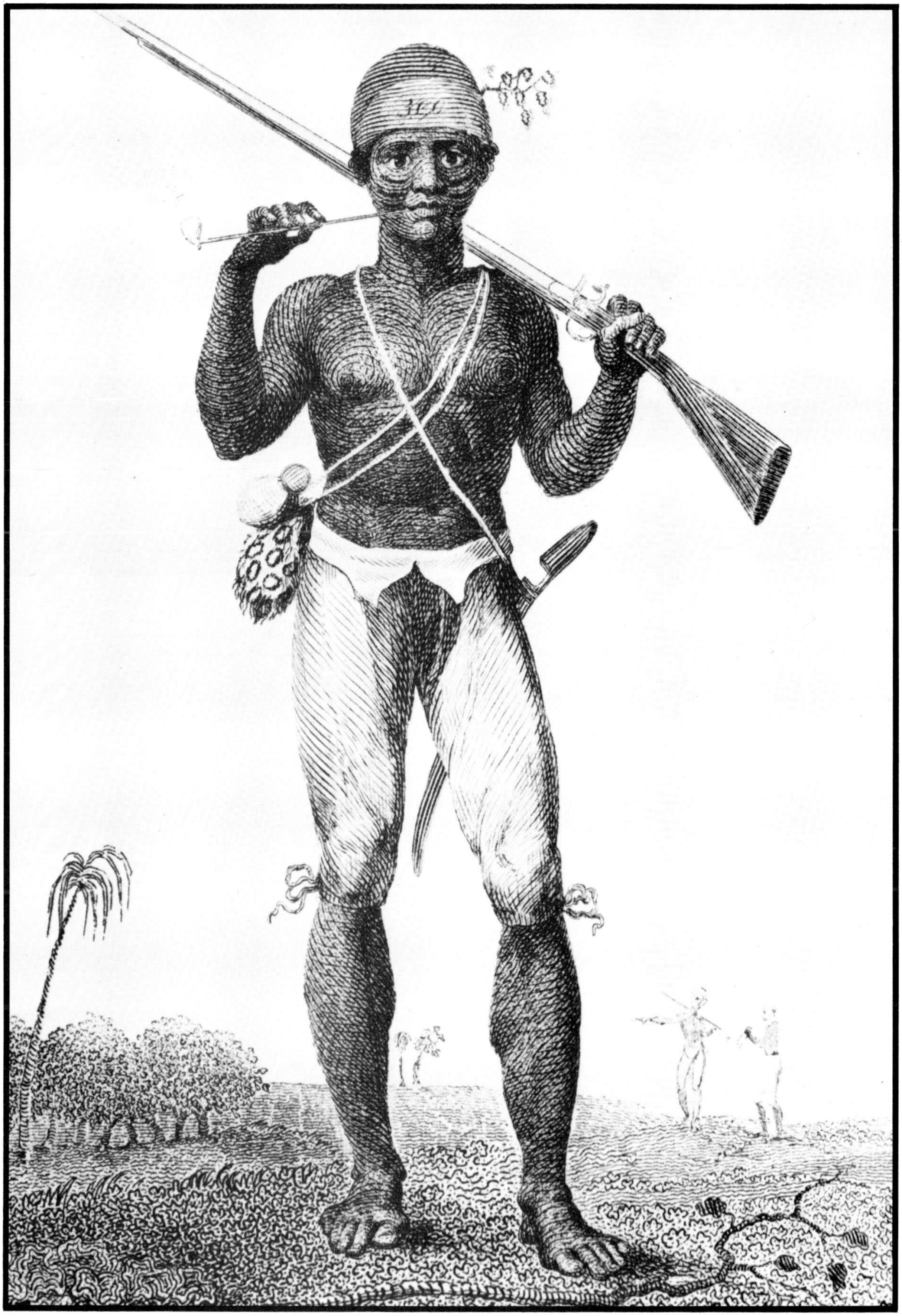

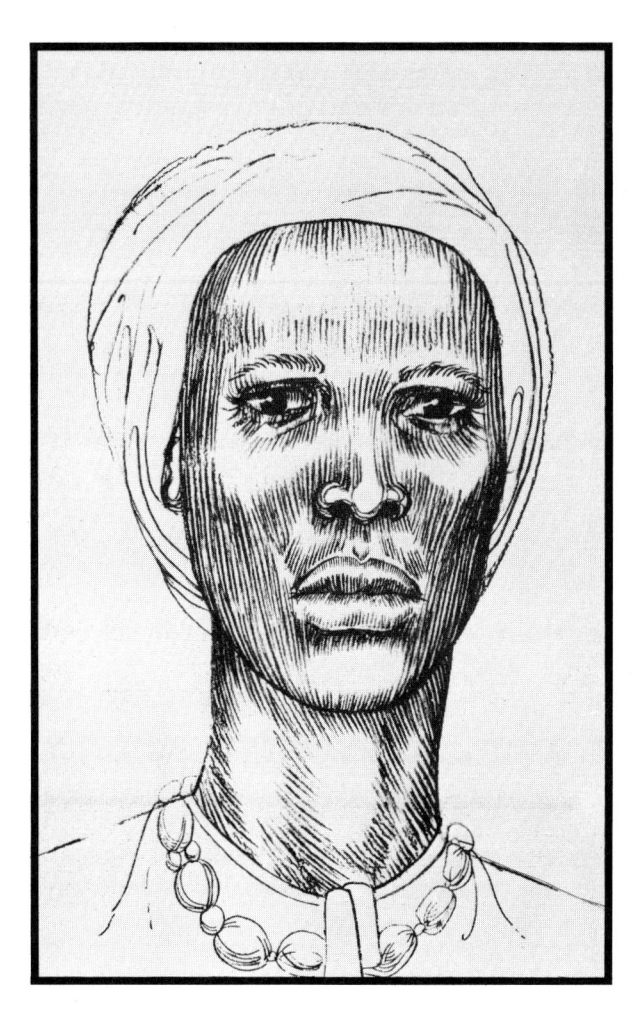

Left – **Nanny of the Maroons**. Below – **Kumina dancers**. Facing, Top – **Trinity Estate St. Mary's**. Facing, Bottom – **Holland Estate**.

'the practice of bush medicine') to treat sick slaves on the plantations. According to some accounts, the legendary Maroon 'Nanny' was a Myal woman who performed such healing services, in addition to leading her people's rebellious struggle. Nanny is also said to have possessed extraordinary supernatural powers through Myal; and that she and some of her comrades used Myal medicines to make themselves invulnerable to the invading English soldiers' bullets. There are even stories of certain slave masters enjoying the benefits of Myal medicine, which they acquired through the generosity of some slave who had access to it.

Myalism quickly spread to the plantation and became the religion of the slaves. However, the cult was forbidden by the masters, who feared that the unifying potential of the ceremonies might encourage slaves to revolt. Indeed, laws were enacted (around 1774) prescribing the death sentence for anyone attending Myal ceremonies. But this did not deter the African slaves. The Myal cult went underground and became a core element of the slaves' secret religious (and political) activity.

The dance form connected with the Myal ceremony was known as **Kumina**, and this term is now used to describe the original Afro-religious expression of the slaves. A number of Jamaican cultural historians, including Edward Seaga (present Prime Minister) and Olive Lewin, however, argue that Kumina was in fact introduced to Jamaica by free Africans after Emancipation (1838), and that it coincided with the spread of Afro-Christian Revivalism which had occurred during the post-slavery years. Nevertheless, it is certain that some form of Myalism became the slave religion, and this has been classified as Kumina. Kumina is now considered the core of the Afro-Jamaica tradition; and its influence can be felt today in many aspects of Jamaican folk and popular culture.

The Jamaican plantation regime was brutal in the extreme. Slaves were not merely defined as property, they were regarded and exploited as machines. Their sole function was to produce great wealth for the Planter class and, ultimately, for Britain. What's more, the white masters

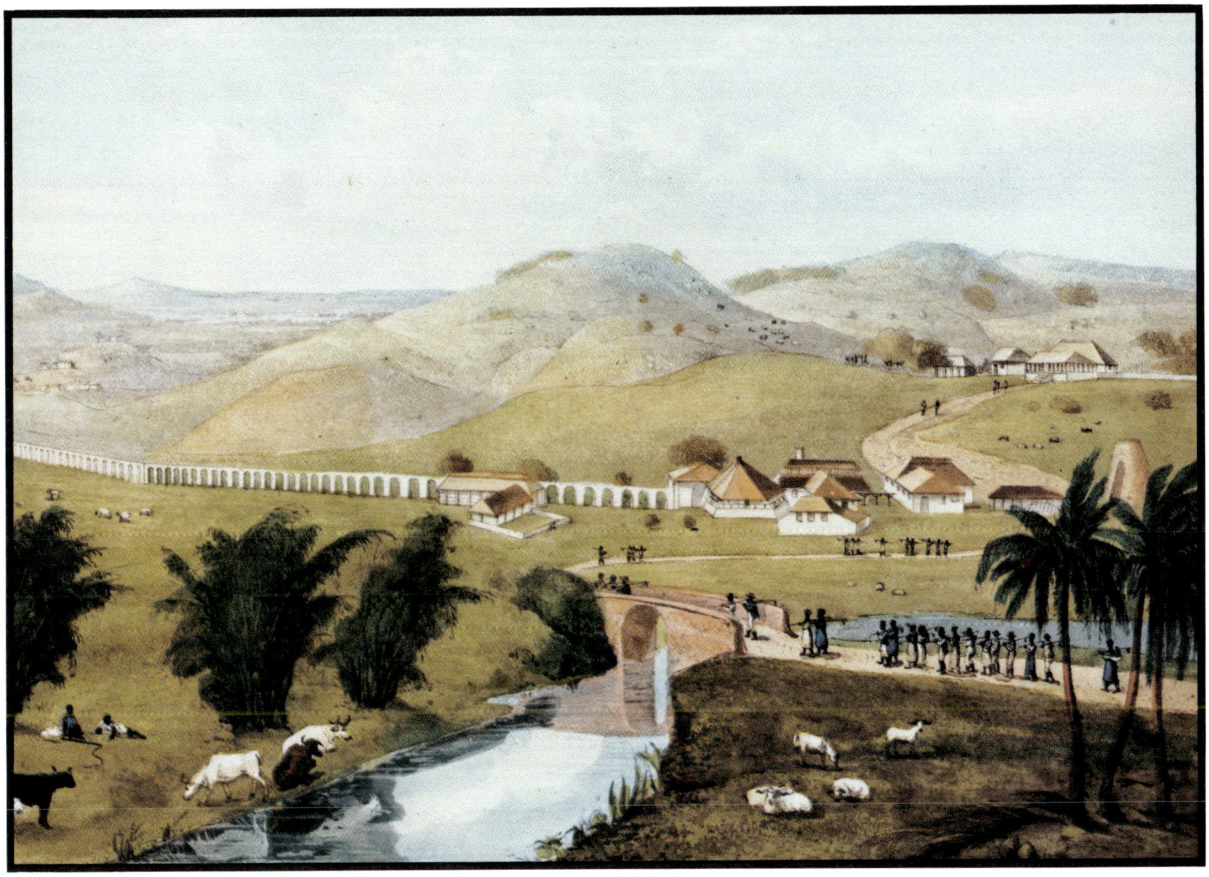

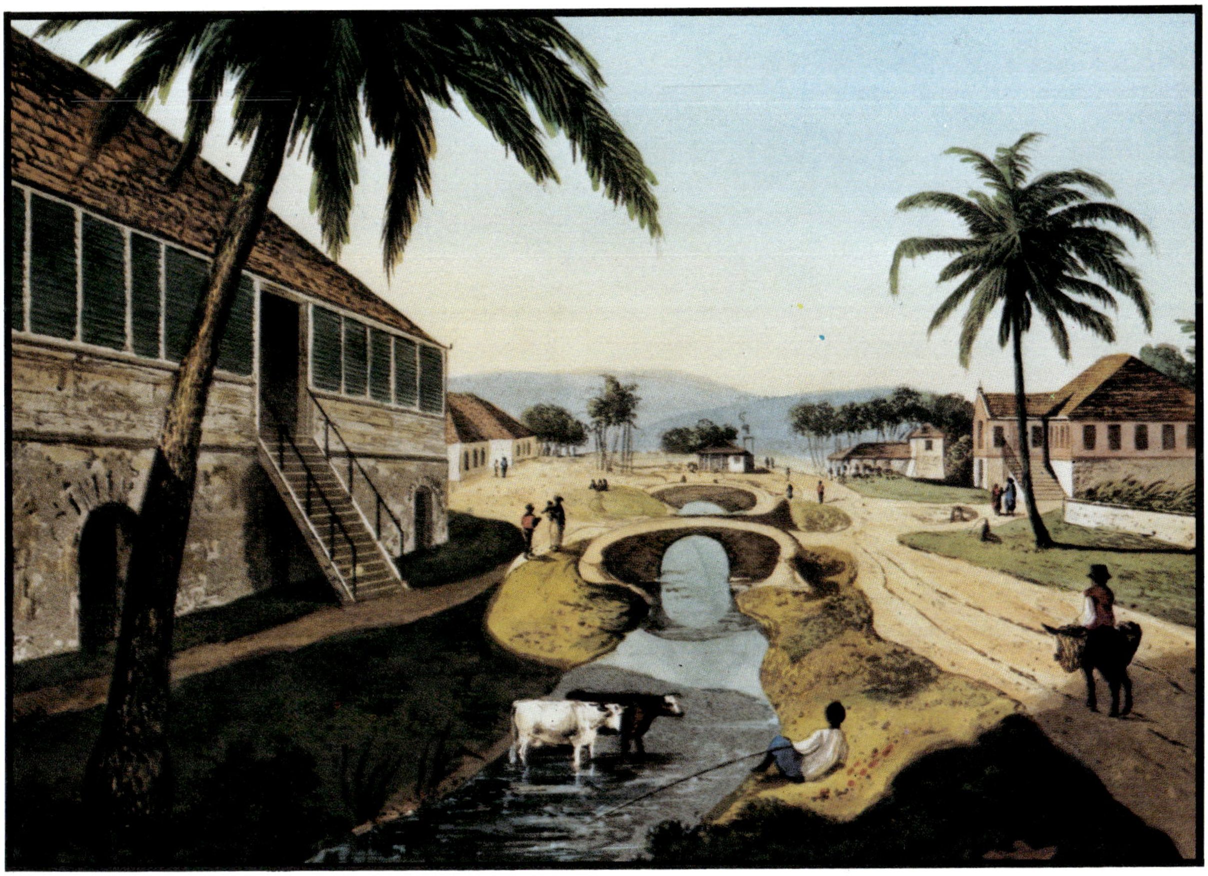

Above – Trelawney Town, the chief Residence of the Maroons. Facing – A Myal man at work.

made no attempt to Christianise their slaves. As they saw it, the Christianisation of the so-called 'heathens', under slavery, was an uneconomic proposition. They also feared that the egalitarian themes expressed in the Bible would incite the slaves to seek their freedom. In any case, the local clergy at the time was notoriously corrupt and decadent, and needed 'saving' itself. This is one of the striking features of Jamaican slavery: a complete absence of a sense of Christian mission among the slave masters, a 'moral' attitude which in other parts of the Caribbean and the United States, usually accompanied the enslavement of the African.

All peoples, whatever their circumstances, create their own systems of beliefs, values and practices – if only in order to structure their lives and define the nature of their relationships with one another. But the Jamaican Planter believed that by reducing the African slaves to machines, he could deprive them of *any* sense of humanity or spirituality. But as it turned out, he only created a cultural vacuum which the slaves quickly filled, using themes and images which they had brought with them from Africa. The slaves fashioned new customs and traditions based on material which they knew and felt best – African philosophy and science, African customs and practices, all the remembered elements of the African world view. So they continued to chant their native chants and sing their native songs, while at work and at play, at times of sorrow and at times of rebellion. They founded a new cultural identity which enabled them to transcend, both spiritually as well as physically, the cruelties of slavery. The free spirit of Myal played a key part in shaping the form and content of this process.

However, the plantation regime limited the chances for purer forms of African slaves' cultural roots, making it exceedingly difficult for a more forceful 'African-ness' to develop within the slave culture of the plantation. But at the same time, slavery did not lead to the complete loss of the slaves' African heritage, as historians argued for many years. On the contrary, there was quite a lot of African-derived activity in the slave quarters, though much of it was necessarily cloaked in secrecy. There was also a great deal of interaction between Maroon communities and the slave population, which meant that a number of important elements of Maroon culture were fed into the culture of the slaves.

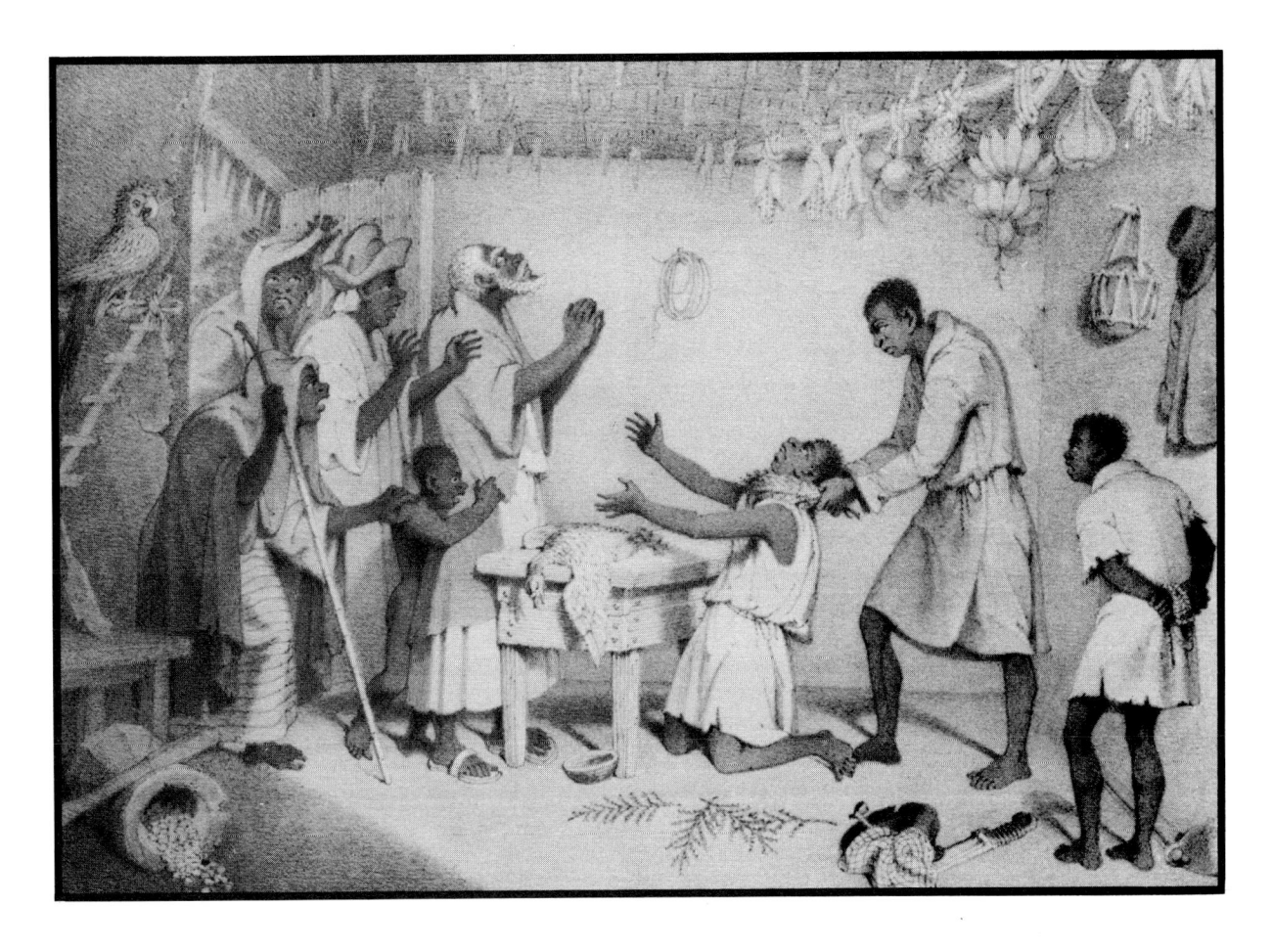

Myal leaders often presided over the secret cult meetings held by the slaves. This was an important channel for transmitting Maroon cultural knowledge to the oppressed population, or at least to sections of it. The religious cult group might also act as the core around which other, more secular activities could be organised – like the planning of rebellions. This shows how the religious and the secular spheres very often overlapped, each sphere giving sustenance to the other. The Myal figure was central to all this, as Garth White points out: 'The Myal man was a medicine man as well as a preacher. He was the man who knew – even though he was transplanted – where to find the correct trees and bushes with which to make medicines. He was also the man who would preside over the sometimes truncated versions of fertility rites. But he was the man who was the central figure on the plantation, around whom the culture was maintained.'

It is not surprising – especially given the break-up of traditional social roles as a result of slavery – that religious expression played such a crucial part in the building of an Afro-Jamaican tradition. As Garth White says: 'You have to take as a given the African attitude to life – which sees religion or things sacred as not specially distinct from the secular. The two merge. So all aspects of their life would be dominated by a concern for the spirits and the ancestors.'

It's worth adding in passing that popular conceptions tend to see only witchcraft (**Obeah**) and spiritualism as being the primary functions of Afro-religious expression. This is a narrow view which neglects the equally important function of this religious form as a powerful social tool, capable of being utilised effectively towards secular ends. The interchangeable roles of the Myal figure is a case in point. At one moment he or she might be a religious-cult leader and practitioner of herbal science, then a musician or dancer providing entertainment or signalling important messages to the people, then helping to organise a slave revolt – all within a relatively short space of time.

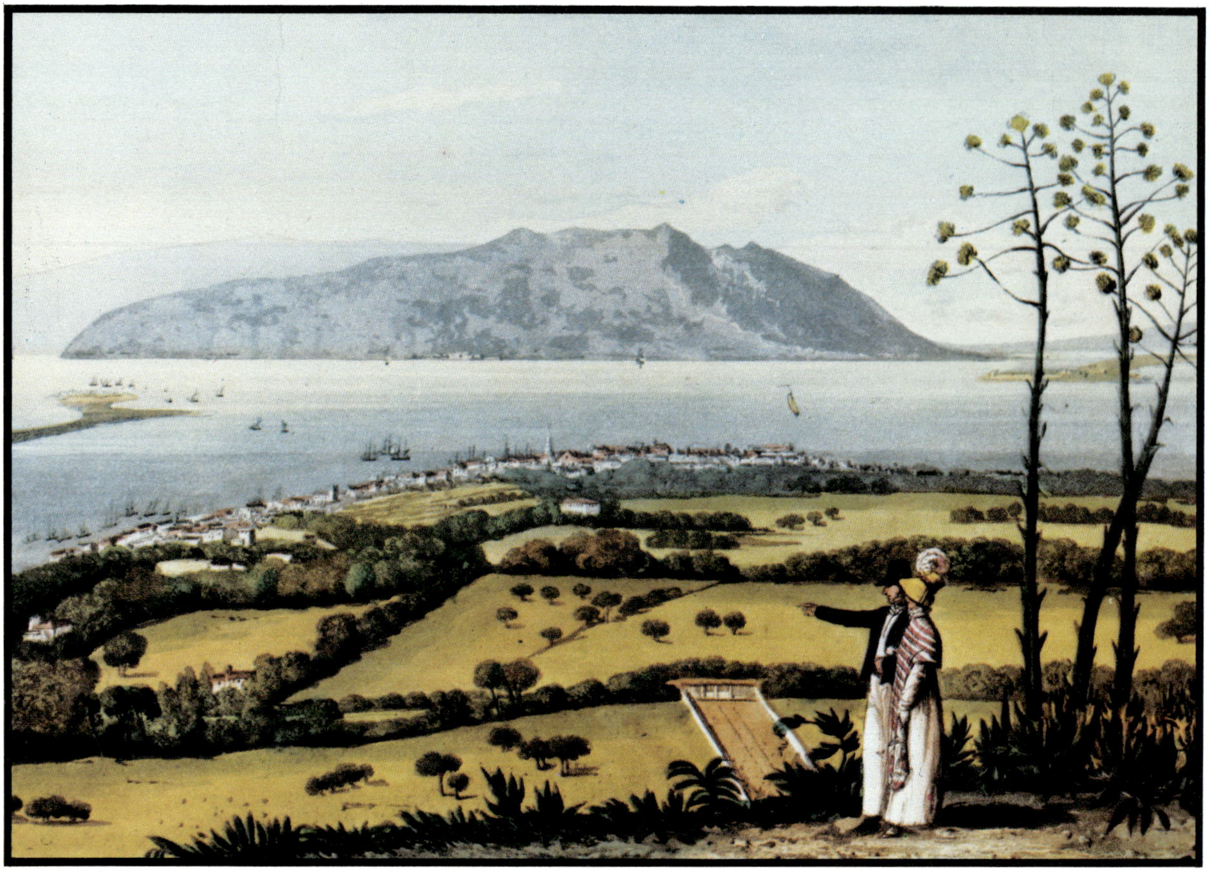

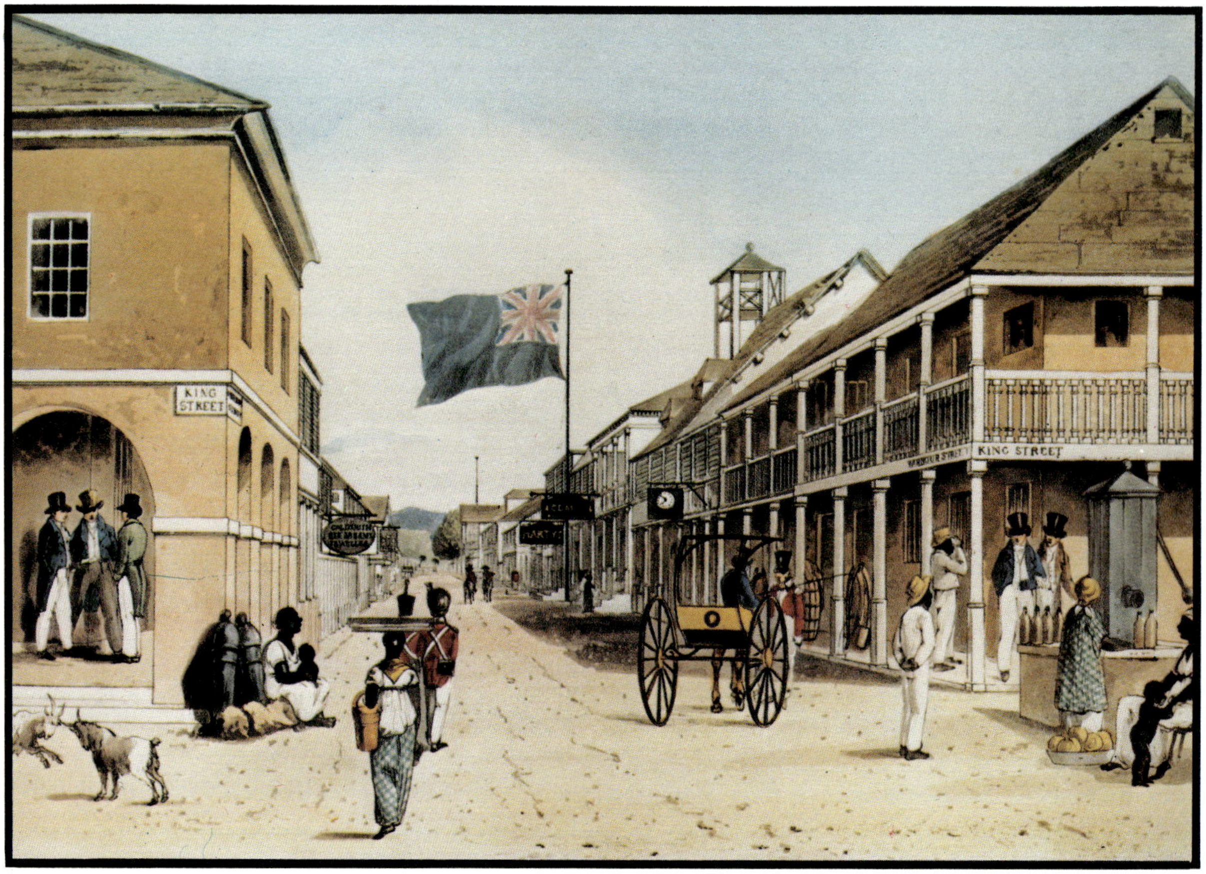
KING STREET
KING STREET

Above – **Pacification with the Maroon Negroes.**
Opposite, Top – **Kingston & Port Royal.** Opposite,
Bottom – **Harbour Street, Kingston.**

The secular tradition: Jonkonnu and Buru

It was through this kind of re-working of traditional social roles, a sort of blending of African-derived customs and beliefs, that the African slaves succeeded in overcoming the oppressive conditions of slavery, and making a resounding impact as a cultural force in the West. It was no mean achievement.

In the African tradition music and dance are inseparable, and with the drum(s) they form an integral part of ceremonial and musical expression. The same applies for the Afro-Jamaican experience, where African survivals are strongly evident in the use of the drum. In earlier times, the Maroons could be heard beating their **Koro** drums from the hilltops at night – which no doubt many slaves on the plantations understood and responded to, while their masters listened in fear. The drum, if you recall, was also used for war in Africa. The plantation owners banned the instrument when they realised that it could be made to 'talk', that the African slaves could communicate with each other via drums and therefore co-ordinate revolt.

Even so, the drum, along with other musical instruments, continued to be used by the slaves. While the Maroons continued to make effective use not only of their African drums, but also of the **Abeng** (or Maroon Horn), sending important signals from the hilltops to the oppressed on the plantation estates. Garth White suggests that there is a close relationship between the musician-drummer and the Myal figure here. Though very often one and the same person (i.e. the Myal cult musician), these two 'seminal characters' played an equally significant part in maintaining and developing the African heritage in Black culture during slavery. They worked hand-in-hand in orchestrating ritual ceremonies of solidarity.

'At first it was only the slaves who were creating the culture. The English Planters at this time had not brought over their own music. What is interesting is that this process repeats itself throughout history, right to this day. In other words, it is the majority of the population – that which was enslaved, now the masses of the population – they are the people who really create the culture. Then in time, rather grudgingly at first, the larger society takes it up as its own,' – Garth White

Alongside the Myal/Kumina religious tradition another, secular, tradition emerged during slavery. This was **Jonkonnu**, a masquerade form that dates back to as early as the 17th century, and survives today as one of the oldest dance forms in Jamaica. Originally, the Jonkonnu (or John Canoe) festival was a religious affair. It employed special songs, drums and drum rhythms, masks and dances, as a means of invoking the spirits. In fact, during the 17th and 18th centuries (at the height of slavery in Jamaica), Jonkonnu was closely related to Myal/Kumina: they both shared the same emphasis on rhythm and percussion, and both were concerned with spirit possession.

But whereas Myal/Kumina was eventually 'driven underground' because of its radical 'African-ness' Jonkonnu, by the 19th century, started to take on more European elements and consequently was allowed to flourish in the open. The original religious significance of Jonkonnu music and dance was lost or submerged, or disguised in symbolism. The traditional characters and themes were made more 'visually acceptable' to European tastes and desires.

Band of the Jaw-Bone John-Canoe.

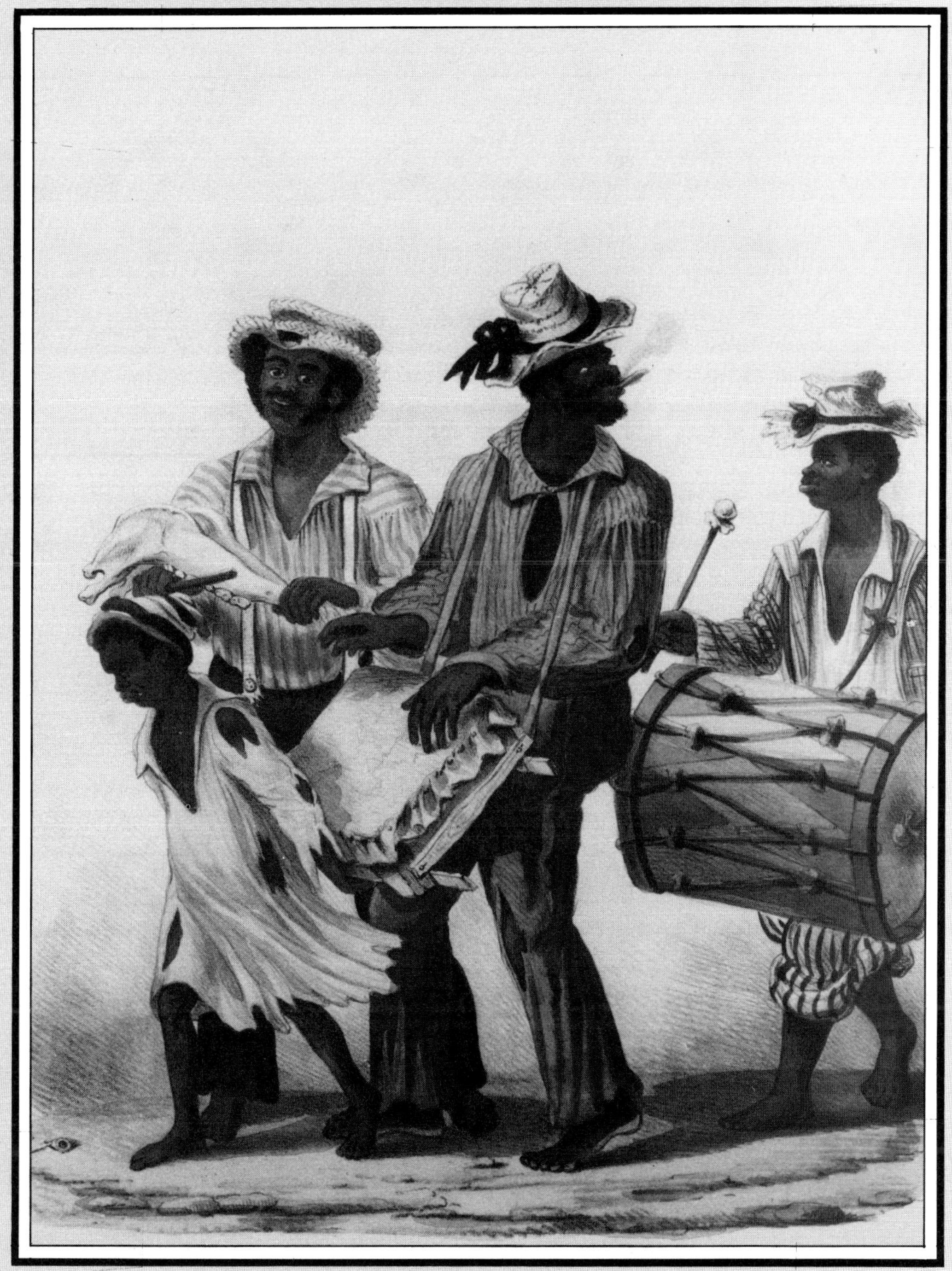

Indeed, the more 'creolised' (or diluted) versions of Jonkonnu, such as the figure dance form known as **Set-Girls**, were encouraged and actively supported by the Planters, and they became a regular feature of plantation entertainment among both the whites and certain slaves.

Although Jonkonnu was absorbed into the dominant plantation culture, certain traditional elements were retained which kept the African connections more or less intact. For example, the emphasis on rhythm and percussion continued to be an integral feature of the performances, though less the possession. Jonkonnu also continued to use the flat, square-shaped **Gumbay** drum, a percussive instrument which was closely associated with the Myal cult. The Gumbay dance is still found in certain Maroon communities, and is considered the purest form of Myalism in Jamaica today.

Left – **Jonkanoo Dancers.** Below – **Lovey.** Bottom – **Koo, Koo, or Actor Boy.**

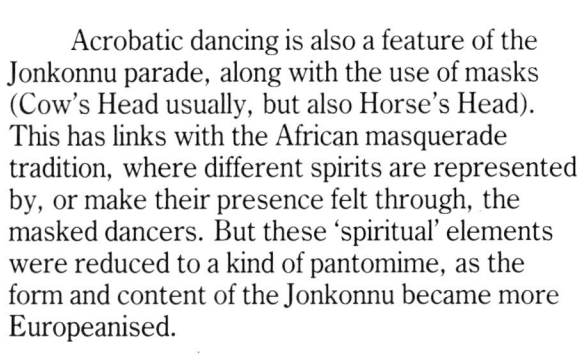

Acrobatic dancing is also a feature of the Jonkonnu parade, along with the use of masks (Cow's Head usually, but also Horse's Head). This has links with the African masquerade tradition, where different spirits are represented by, or make their presence felt through, the masked dancers. But these 'spiritual' elements were reduced to a kind of pantomime, as the form and content of the Jonkonnu became more Europeanised.

Top – Negro Figuranti. Bottom – French Set-Girls.

Olive Lewin suggests that the origins of Jonkonnu have to be looked at from a wider perspective. 'For instance, part of our Jonkonnu tradition,' she points out, 'has to do with plays – plays that seem to have been founded on old English stories about kings and queens and so on. And in the stories there is a death; jostling with swords; then a doctor is sent for – who is our kind of "healer" – and there is a magical return to life. Now, I recently saw exactly that depicted in a Korean traditional group using masks and music. I have also seen similar things in Amerindian culture; they have it in Scandanavia; and I've seen it in Yugoslavia. So when people tell you that Jonkonnu came from such and such a place, that need not be the case. All you can say is that it can also be found in other cultures. You cannot say that Jonkonnu came from a specific place, because it could be just a manifestation of some *human* need for a particular type of outpouring. It could have come from many different places.'

The change in the Jamaican Jonkonnu – from its original religious function to a more secularized form of entertainment – occurred with the introduction of the **Set-Girls**. 'The Set-Girls,' as Garth White explains, 'were groups of ladies who provided entertainment for visiting military personnel. What happened was that there was a meeting between the Set-Girls form and Jonkonnu. Jonkonnu had developed a masquerade tradition, where the performers would travel to different plantations giving entertainment. The Set-Girls also had a masquerade tradition; they would march through the streets and down to the waterfront, where they would vie with one another. You would have different coloured "Sets" – a "Red Set", a "Blue Set" and so on – each representing a particular branch of the armed forces, for example. When the two traditions came together – which was probably pushed by the white power structure at the time – the Set-Girls came to have a predominance over the Jonkonnu performance. But as I've said before, whatever happens, you always have a true line. So when the Set-Girls disappeared you found that Jonkonnu was still there. In fact it is still with us now.'

But the different coloured 'Sets' was more than mere theatrical display; it also reflected the colour caste structure of Jamaican society. In other words, the Set-Girls were also graded according to the shade of their complexion. 'Black' girls did not dance with 'Brown' girls; the 'creole' Black-Sets (i.e. Afro-Jamaicans) were separate from the 'African' Brown-Sets (i.e. slaves born in Africa). It was a clear-cut arrangement: the whites at the top of the social-cum-racial ladder, the Blacks at the bottom, with the middle left pretty much to the 'Brown' girls to battle it out.

It would be unfair to dismiss Jonkonnu simply as a product of white domination, however. Accepting that it had lost its religious significance, it nevertheless continued to perform an important social function. At the very least, it brought the various social groupings – represented by 'sets' of dancers – together under one, communal banner. In this respect, Jonkonnu followed the Carnival tradition very closely; it provided an opportunity for the oppressed people to dress up and play at being kings and queens, lords and ladies, and through these roles mock the status quo. In a less extravagant fashion, the Jamaican **Quadrille** dance served the same purpose.

The Quadrille was a group ballroom set dance which was popular in Europe in the late-18th to 19th centuries. It originated in France and was taken up by the English Court,

31

and from there it was taken to Jamaica (and other slave colonies) by the plantation owners. It was danced by the plantation gentry, and eventually filtered down to the slave population by way of their participation as musicians. The dance was transformed by the Black population, where it exhibited more 'the distinctive "African" bounce quality' for which it is noted, as well as an expressive tone of derision.

Another secular form which had emerged during the slavery period was **Buru** music. Like Jonkonnu, with which it is closely associated, the Buru began as a religious form, then gradually became more secularized. It was originally a fertility masquerade dance; and though the masquerade element was lost, the fertility aspect persisted in the form of 'provocative' dance movements, and in the music's characteristic 'earthiness'. Buru did not suffer the same degree of dilution as Jonkonnu.

The Buru is said to have been one of the few African forms of music that was allowed by the slave master. Buru bands, according to some accounts, were allowed to play their music in the fields, to help the slaves work faster! This sounds pretty far-fetched; but then the plantation system did produce curious anomalies. Garth White puts a more positive light on the matter, however, when he points out that black musicians at the time tended to 'duplicate their services'. In other words, 'the white man could not deny the beauty of our music. So while he fought against the underground cult activity, and while he wouldn't countenance in hearing any drums beating or "noise making" as he called it, he still had to organise groups of musicians to entertain him.' Consequently, the slave musician found himself working in two, quite contradictory social and musical settings – he would be providing entertainment for the white master in the Great House at one moment, then performing at secret cult meetings and inspiring solidarity among the slaves the next.

The 'Buru man' is reputed to have been held in low esteem by the rest of the community at the time, possibly because his music was so strongly associated with violence and eroticism, and as such considered vulgar. Yet these negative associations do not tally with the popularity which the Buru musician seems to have enjoyed at the time, and the influence that Buru music has had on the contemporary folk and popular traditions, especially on Rastafarian music since the 1940s.

Opposite – Slaves entertain themselves for the moment on the plantation. Above – Quadrille Dancers.

Buru music, like its religious counterpart, Kumina, is very much rooted in the African heritage. But unlike Kumina, which is concerned mainly with ancestral spirits and unites the community through worship and possession ('to catch Myal'), Buru is part of the African musical tradition of social commentary and satire. In this respect, it is similar to aspects of Jonkonnu. After Emancipation, Buru musicians became closely connected with Christmas festivities, where their songs would recount the past year's events that had affected the community. During the 1940's, when Buru music was very popular in the Kingston ghettoes, families would hire a Buru man to play at the welcoming of released prisoners back into the community.

Veteran drummer Skully recounts how 'the buru man would go to the penitentiary gate, and play that you hear prisoner inside call out man name. And the man on the street, the buru man, would answer him and say, "Boy, I know you soon come out, but I just a-chant you out." So him just play upon him drum and chant him some hymns. Yeah, buru man say (sings), "Clap your tiny hands, clap your tiny hands, clap your tiny hands for Jah." '

At the other end of the scale, Buru performers made effective use of songs of derision, in which they would often criticise important figures in the community, or pick on a resident who had committed some misdeed. Significantly, the 'victims' of these musical jibes would have the option of returning the gestures, also through song. This ability to cast public shame on the 'guilty' person, suggests that the Buru man might have had an important moral function to play in the community, reminding people of their good points as well as their bad. If so, it was more a social kind of morality, than religious.

Buru music places strong emphasis on song, or on the vocal aspect of musical expression. A number of percussive instruments provide the rhythmic support – including the Bamboo Scraper, Shakka and Rhumba Box (i.e. the Jamaican equivalent of the African thumb piano). This may have been the traditional Buru set-up, and it is significant that all these instruments are highly portable. Perhaps only later did Buru become more closely associated with the drum. Many Jamaicans who grew up in the 1940s still recall 'the earthy ridims of the Buru' that would fill the night air. Rhythmic playing, singing or dancing of any kind was apparently referred to as 'Buru' during this period. It was the 'Buru drum' that greatly influenced later developments in Jamaican popular music.

Jamaican musicologists and cultural historians have pointed out the close relationship between Buru, Kumina and Rasta music – particularly in the types of drums each uses, and their respective drumming rhythms (or ridims). Buru music, as we mentioned, emphasises the vocal element, with the accompaniment of fairly simple percussive instruments. The Buru drums – i.e. the **Fundeh** and the **Repeater** – subsequently came more to the fore; and it was the Buru ridims that were absorbed into Rasta. As Olive Lewin notes: 'If you slow down Buru,

Negro dance.

you can sometimes hear Rasta music.'

In Kumina music, drumming ridims play a crucial part in the ceremony, driving the Kumina dancers steadily but dramatically towards possession. Here only two drums are employed: the **Kbandu**, which provides the bass rhythm; and the **Playing Cast** (or lead drum), on which very complex rhythms are beat out in a quick tempo. Kumina music also makes important use of **Katta** ridims or sticks played on the open end of one of the drums; this gives the sense of three percussive instruments backing the Kumina performance. Several subsidiary percussive items such as the Grater and Shakkas may also be included in the instrumentation.

Rasta music, though religious in orientation, found its strongest musical impulse in secular Buru ridims. Significantly, Rasta drums are called 'a Buru set'. Rasta and Buru are closely related, however, not only in terms of their drumming patterns, but also in their similar use of social commentary and satire in the lyrics, although Rasta drew equally from the Kumina tradition, which is reflected in its emphasis on 'Africanness' and spirituality. In terms of instrumentation, too, Rasta represents an advance on earlier forms, using a basic set-up of three traditional drums – the **Bass Drum**; the **Fundeh**, which is related to the Kbandu of Kumina; and the **Repeater (peta)**, which is closer to the Playing Cast of the Kumina. Rasta music has a slower tempo than Kumina and Buru as well.

The advent of Buru music clearly shows the extent to which the African slaves had drawn on the secular, as distinct from the religious, elements of their cultural heritage. The tradition was maintained through slavery by the Buru man, whose somewhat unusual position in the plantation setting probably enabled him to avoid major influences from outside and dilutions of the form. The tradition continued long after emancipation and well into the 1940s, again aided no doubt by the Buru man's unconventional position in Jamaican society as a wandering or self-employed musician. In many respects, the Buru man is a prototype of the contemporary Afro-Jamaican musician.

MURDER
OF
ELEVEN WOMEN
IN THE WEST INDIES.

(Extract from Lord Brougham's Speech in the House of Lords, February 20, 1838.)

"ELEVEN Females have been flogged, starved, lashed, attached to the Tread-mill, and compelled to work, until nature could no longer endure their sufferings. At the moment when the wretched victims were about to fall off,—when they could no longer bring down the mechanism, and continue the movement,—they were suspended by their arms, and at each revolution of the wheel received new wounds on their members, until, in the language of that law so grossly outraged in their persons, they 'languished and died.' Ask you if a crime of this murderous nature went unvisited, and if no inquiry was made respecting its circumstances? The forms of justice were observed;—the handmaid was present, but the sacred mistress was far away. A coroner's inquest was called; for the laws declared that no such injuries should take place without having an inquiry instituted. Eleven inquisitions were held,—eleven inquiries were made,—eleven verdicts were returned —for Murder?—Manslaughter?—Misconduct?—No! but that '*they died by the visitation of God*'!—A Lie!—A Perjury!—A Blasphemy!"

Do you doubt the truth of these appalling facts? Do you imagine that the statement must be exaggerated? What was the reply of the Colonial Secretary? Lord Glenelg admitted "that the great extent of evil under the Apprenticeship system, which Lord Brougham had stated, DID exist, and that his noble friend had NOT exaggerated those evils." He allowed "that the most horrid cruelties were perpetrated in the West Indies"—"scenes on which it was impossible for the mind to dwell without horror."

BRITONS! shall these horrors continue? Not while you have hearts to feel, and voices to plead for the oppressed. Come, instantly, and sign Petitions to Parliament, respectfully, but most earnestly praying for the IMMEDIATE, COMPLETE, UNCONDITIONAL Freedom of the wretched Negro-Apprentices. "There is only ONE remedy for the evils of slavery, and that remedy is **PERFECT FREEDOM!!**"

We Need A Revival

For a long time, Christianity made little impression on Jamaican slave culture. As we discussed earlier, the English Planters were not interested in converting their slaves, only in working them. This resulted in the slaves developing their own religious practices, based on their African background. It is possible, of course, that a few elements of Christian religion seeped into the slave community via house servants, for example. Through their closer contacts with the master, these slaves, perhaps less harassed than those in the field, would have had greater opportunity to acquire bits of Christian knowledge. But it is doubtful that this was widespread.

As for missionaries, the Moravians had arrived in Jamaica in 1734, followed by the Methodists two years later. They both were interested in 'the welfare of the slaves' and certainly tried to influence affairs. But neither of them really succeeded in building a significant following, although the Methodists did make some gains on which they were able to capitalise in later years.

Ironically, it was an Afro-American Baptist preacher, George Liele (sometimes spelt Lisle), who succeeded in establishing a foothold in the island and opened the way for Christian ideas to spread among the Jamaican slaves. Liele had already built himself a reputation as a slave preacher in Georgia, where he founded a Baptist church in 1779, before coming to Jamaica with a white patron to settle. And in 1784, he founded the first Baptist church in the island, which he named the Ethiopian Baptist church.

Liele's form of Gospel was unique and vibrant: it combined Christian concepts with strong elements of African-derived rituals and beliefs. It was an Afro-Christian form of worship; it accepted the basic precepts of Christian belief, while at the same time giving full expression to black spirituality. This appealed to the slaves, whose own religion was rooted in the African heritage. Here, they were able to take on the Christian God and the Trinity, and still maintain their own religious and ceremonial traditions. Thus invocation and possession, music and dance, remained central even within this Christianised form of worship.

These Afro-Christian followers came to be known as **Native Baptists**. Like the Myal/Kumina leaders and cults before them, Native Baptist preachers and congregations of the 19th century became the focus of much social and political activity. Prayer meetings, like secret cult meetings, became important occasions – where the spirit of freedom and rebellion kindled, and strategies for revolt materialised. This was the setting in which such figures as Samuel Sharpe, himself a Baptist preacher, succeeded in building an effective, slave-directed struggle against slavery.

The Emancipation of the slaves in 1834 naturally began a new chapter in Jamaican social and cultural history. A new optimism was felt, as the freed slaves moved off the plantations to establish homesteads in relatively isolated rural parts of the island. This was the beginning of the Jamaican peasantry. But though their new situation was a definite improvement on slavery, they still had to face the difficult task of adjustment. The strains and pressures that ensued are thought to have contributed to the outbreak of **Obeah** (sorcery) and the resurgence of Myal cult activity. These developments led to the Myal Procession of 1842, which was joined by many Native Baptists as well as Orthodox

Extract from Lord Brougham's speech re Freedom of Slaves.

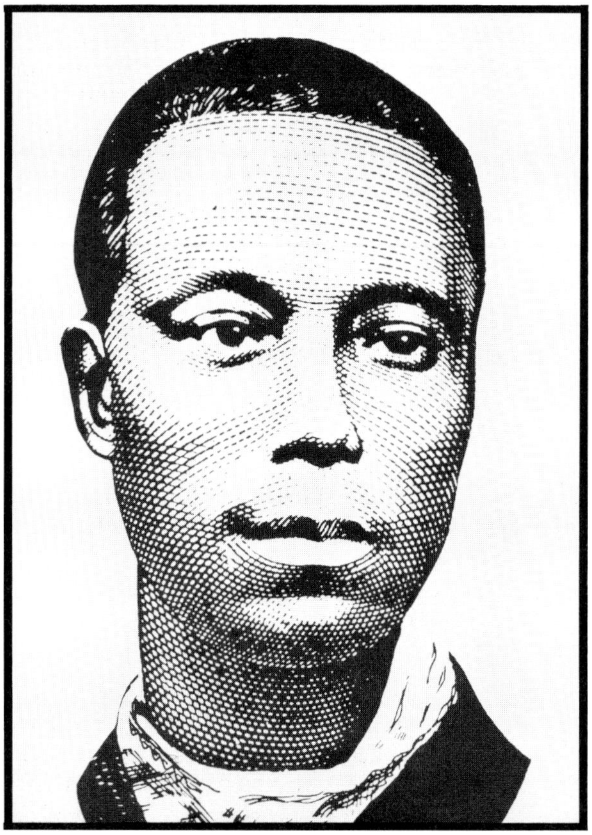

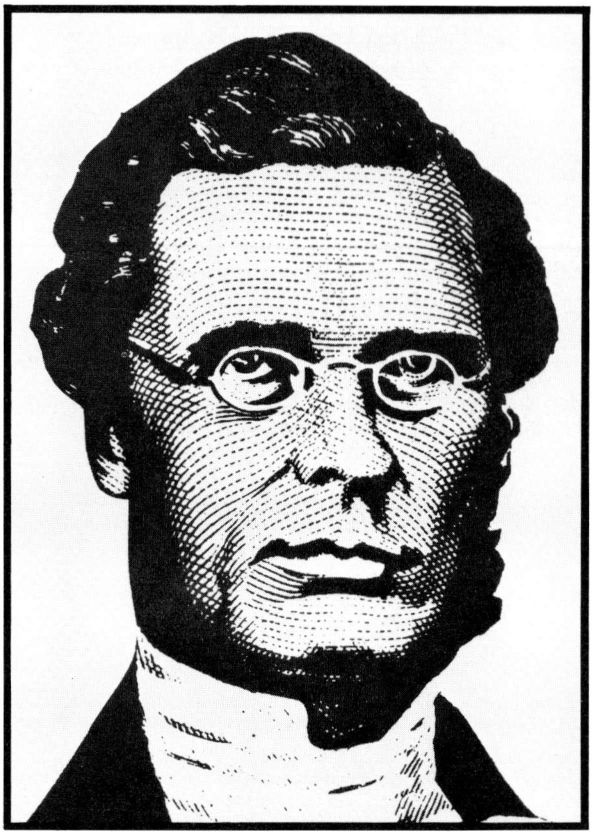

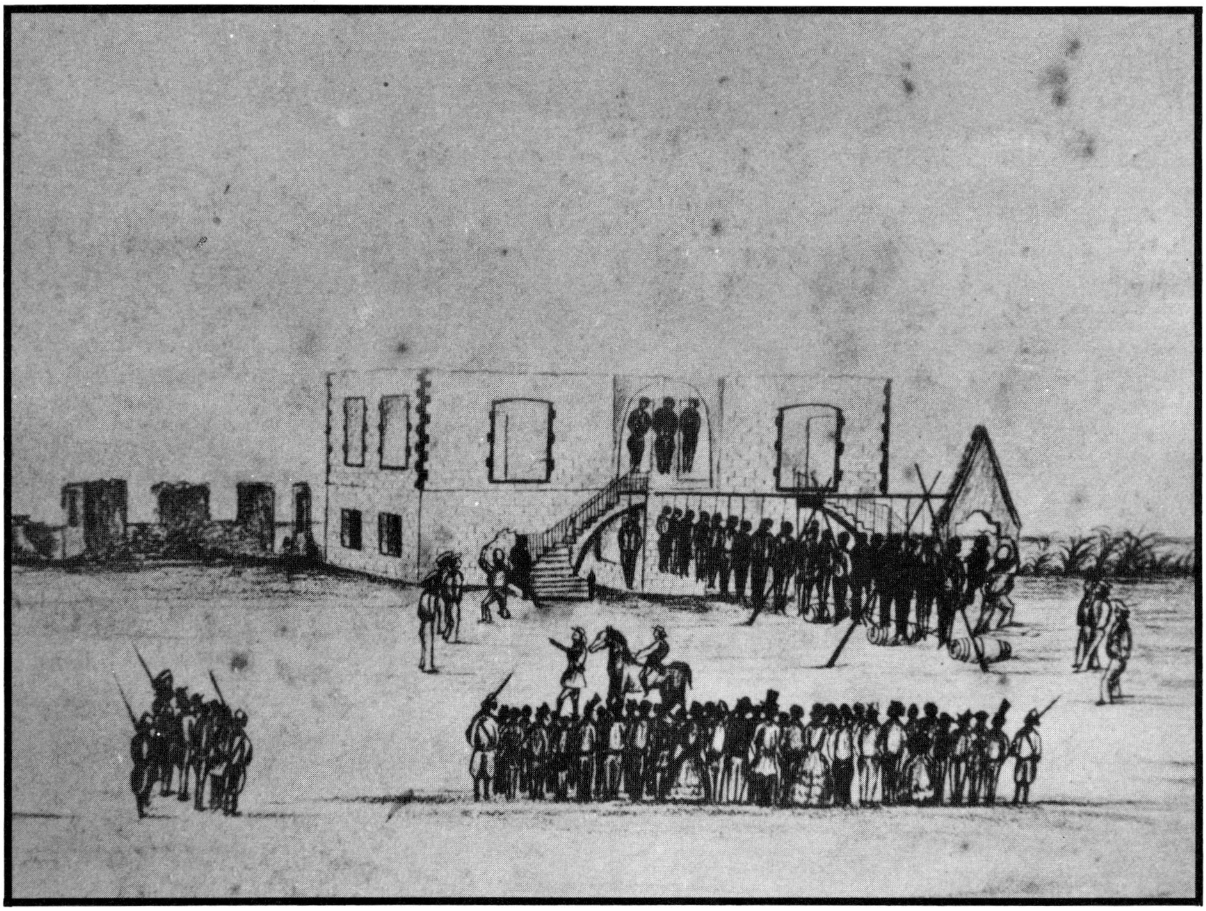

Opposite, Top – **Paul Bogle and George William Gordon**, ministers of the Native Baptists Church of Jamaica, were both hung for the famous Morante Bay rebellion in 1865. Opposite, Bottom – The hanging of Paul Bogle. Left – Sam Sharpe's rebellious activities hastened the emancipation of slaves, although he was executed in 1832 two years before the full abolition.

Baptists.

This upsurge in religious activity led to one of the most spectacular religious phenomena to occur in Jamaican history – The Great Revival of 1860-61. Although it was started by Orthodox Christian missionaries (following the examples of Revivalism which had just occurred in the United States and Britain), the Jamaican Great Revival was soon taken over by Native Baptists and Myal groups, who turned it into an expression of Afro-Christian dynamism. Thousands of people flocked to the churches, to take part in the resurgence of spirituality that swept across the island.

The Great Revival gave birth to two main branches of Revivalism or Afro-Christian sects in Jamaica: **Pukkumina** and **Zion Revival**. The difference between the two is one of emphasis. Pukkumina has retained strongly African-derived elements in its rituals and beliefs, whereas Zion Revival is more Christian in orientation. But Revivalism generally, including both Pukkumina and Zion cults, diverges from the orthodox or established Christian churches in a fundamental way.

For example, the established church recognises only one deity; whereas Revival not only accepts the Christian Trinity, the Angels and Apostles but also believes in 'a pantheon of spirits' which can affect the living directly. The belief that these spirits (which include the ancestral dead) can be manipulated through invocation, is fundamental to Revival religion. Possession is therefore an integral feature of Revival cult worship. The spirits make their presence felt in a variety of ways. For instance, the physical state of the possessed provides clear signs (to the participants) of which spirits are in action and the depth of the possession. Speaking or singing in 'unknown tongues' is another important form of possession behaviour. This 'language' is made up of 'nonsense syllables' which, according to a number of authorities, contain African words with which the possessed is otherwise unfamiliar. Singing, dancing, rhythmic accompaniment such as drumming, clapping, stamping, 'groaning' or over-breathing, all play an essential part in the Revival ceremony.

To a greater or lesser extent, Revival re-works the 'accepted' themes and images of Christian religion, in order that worship should retain and revitalise a fundamental sense of Black Spirituality. Garth White sees this process as being historically significant, as well as culturally:

'Revival is always close to Black people in Jamaica, whether they are believers or non-believers. In fact, every little community has its clap-hand church, where you see that people have not really let go of this spiritual dimension. So they will hold on to a Supreme Being; but it cannot be the lily-white God-head that seems not to like movement (to put it charitably). They could only take on a religion in which this Supreme Being also manifested his power in a number of other spirits, and who was not averse to singing and dancing. This was in keeping with their African traditions – where music and dance were not seen in strictly secular terms. And this is probably what prevented the white man from really ever penetrating and killing off (as he did so many other things) our musical culture. He could never determine what was sacred from what was secular. This was especially important during slavery, because the spiritual food that the slaves got from music and dance encouraged their sense of solidarity and, in fact, cemented bonds across the plantations.'

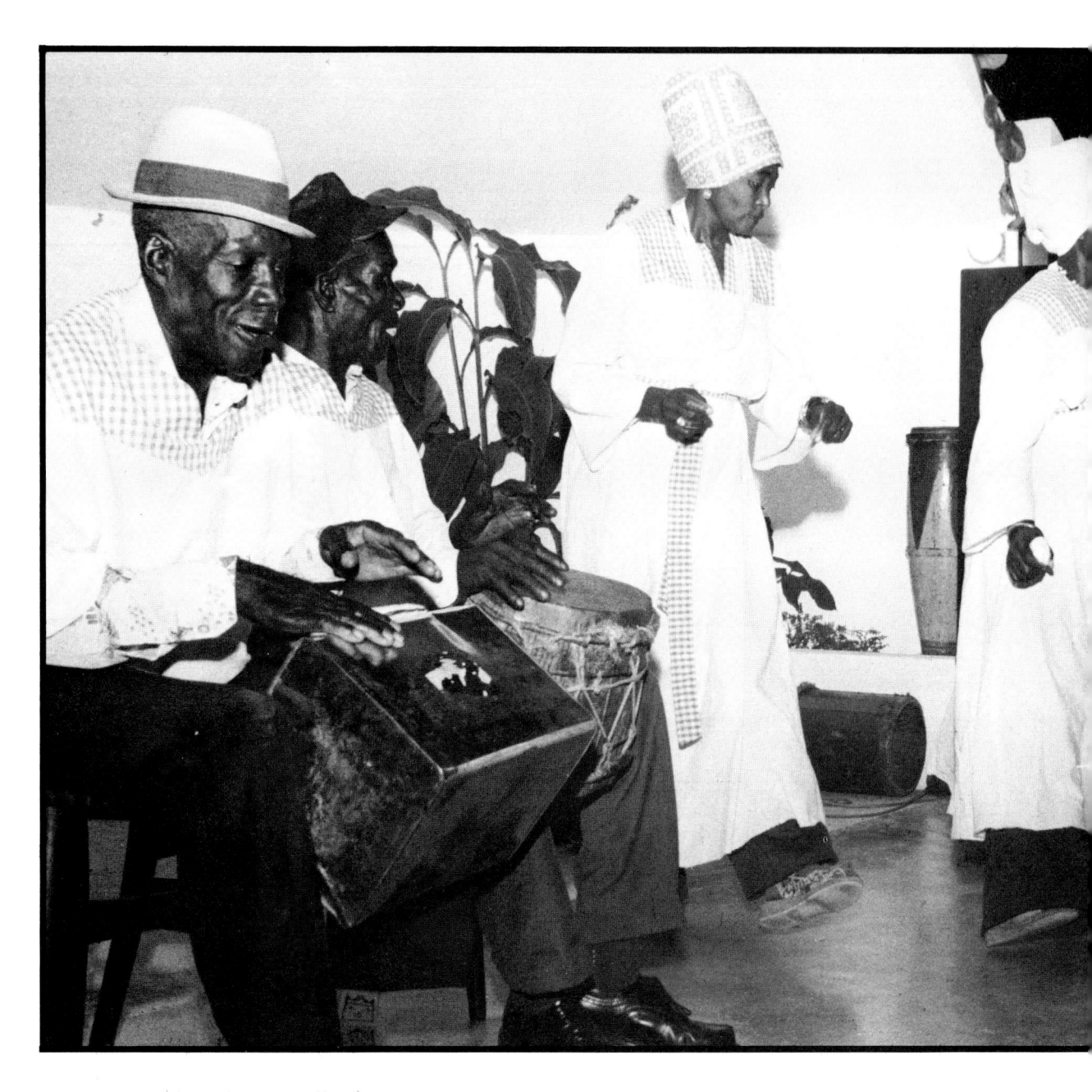

The strong differences between the established church on the one hand, and the 'marginal' Revival cults on the other, would suggest that these two styles of worship are incompatible. But, as Pamela O'Gorman points out, there is a tendency for people to belong to both: 'There has always been a kind of ambivalence in Jamaica towards what is established and what is of the roots. People have belonged to one of the established churches, and at the same time have belonged to a Pukkumina group or a Revival group or a Kumina group. It is a way of playing on both sides of the fence – if one side doesn't work, they will try the other. So you find that while people will go to the Methodist or Baptist church on Sunday – particularly if they are in trouble – they will also arrange a Kumina to fix up the same trouble. This is part of the whole process, a most exciting process in the Caribbean, in which you will find people subscribing to Western values on the one

Pukkumina dancers.

hand, and subscribing to African values on the other.'

The Zion form of Revival is less rooted in the African tradition and emphasises European-Christian elements more strongly, than the Pukkumina form. 'Most of the hymns that are sung in Zion,' notes Pamela O'Gorman, 'are European. Of course the performance style of these hymns are going to be quite different, and will owe much to the African background. But apart from the percussion and the rather open-voiced style of singing, Zion Revival is most strongly on the European side of the continuum.' In contrast, Pukkumina is part of the strongly African-derived cultural tradition which includes Myal and Kumina. To use Olive Lewin's words, 'Kumina and Pukkumina come from broadly the same world view.'

Pukkumina is customarily referred to as 'Pocomania'. But Olive Lewin and others have pointed out that this is an inappropriate term. It is a translation of two Spanish words, 'Poco' (little) and 'mania' (madness) – hence 'a little madness'. There are at least two reasons why this form of Revival should not be called 'Pocomania' or 'a little madness'. Firstly, Jamaican Revival has no links with Spanish culture; so the word itself bears no relation to the origins of the religion. Olive Lewin suggests that 'Pocomania' is in fact an Anglicised version of 'Pukkumina' – which makes the concidence with 'a little madness' even more sinister.

Secondly, many people in that part of Revival do not use the term 'Pocomania' to describe themselves. They are aware of its negative meaning and, consequently, will often not even admit to belonging to that system of beliefs. 'Pukkumina', which they do use, is the more appropriate description and is clearly linked to 'Kumina' the root form. It is this sort of confusion or mis-representation, Olive Lewin argues, that we have to begin to correct, as we develop more knowledge about ourselves and our past. But at an even more fundamental level, if Pukkumina is 'a manifestation of deep-seated beliefs that we respect, then we don't want to call it "a little madness".'

Up until about ten or twelve years ago, Pukkumina did not use drums, in contrast to Zion Revivalists, for whom drumming has always been an important element. They would use instead 'body sounds' – such as clapping, stamping, over-breathing, and so on – for rhythmic (percussive) support. 'If they had an Indian band present,' notes Olive Lewin, 'they would use

Revival dancers.

Indian percussive instruments such as the little **mancura** and perhaps a **tabla**.' Today, drums are used in Pukkumina, and they play an integral part in the overall rhythmic structure of the ceremony. As Olive Lewin again describes:

'One of the characteristics of Pukkumina is the 1-2/1-2 etc. beat. This is used in the over-blowing or over-breathing which induces the trance (possession) state in the person, it is also in the stamping and in the chorus. You have a Drum that provides this basic 1-2/1-2... beat, though it may be embellished with other off-beat phrases. Then there is the Side Drum, which provides the more decorative sounds at a higher pitch. Now, these two drums really relate to male and female. This is something that a lot of people do not realise. Because in the world view, you cannot have life without the male and female being represented: spirit-matter, earth-air, and so on. They are complementary. So you will not get a Pukkumina meeting with only one drum present – because you cannot get life or anything good that way, it won't reach the Creator that way.'

The significance of Revival in the Jamaican folk tradition cannot be overstated. Indeed, it is virtually impossible to separate the two – the religious and the folk are integral parts of the same universe, each draws on the other to sustain the whole. And as Pamela O'Gorman's next example shows, this also lies at the roots of Jamaican popular music: 'In the early days of reggae' she notes, 'when you had the **Ska**, most of the dance steps were Pukkumina dance steps. It's a beautiful thing, that you can take a traditional religious form like Pukkumina and transplant it to a modern, urban form – and nobody thought that there was any strangeness about this at all. It demonstrates the beautiful way in which Jamaicans mould the secular and the religious.'

From his own researches and experience as a producer in the early days of reggae, Edward Seaga concurs with Pamela O'Gorman's observation. 'The folk and religious tradition,' he says, 'forms part of the rhythmic base in popular music. In many instances, it forms a part of the songs, the melodies and the lyrics. Some folk tunes have been taken and performed in another rhythmic style as popular music. But in other instances, it has contributed by way of inspiration. Artists like Toots and the Maytals and Prince Buster draw heavily on this background.'

Folklorist Louise Bennett traces the roots of reggae back to the **Dinkie-Minnie**, an African-derived folk form which was concerned with cheering up the family of the bereaved. 'This happened all during slavery,' she says, 'and it was one occasion where the slaves were free to really express themselves.' It is worth interjecting here the fact that the death rate among slaves was frighteningly high. Funeral occasions were thus very frequent in the slave community, and no doubt they were tinged with anger as the slaves saw their friends and loved ones dying at the hands of the white slave master. These otherwise sad occasions provided a context in which the slaves met regularly, could reassess their situation, and plan counter-measures.

'The whole ritual of the dinkie-minnie,' continues Louise Bennett, 'has a strong therapeutic function which our people in Jamaica used, and it is used in Africa. Its function is to banish sorrow and to prevent the family from grieving – when I say grieving, you are aware of the tragedy but you don't let it overpower you. There is no inward grieving, you dance it off, you move it off. The dinkie-minnie is full of movement.

'You hear a lot of people say, "Oh, the trouble with us is that we really haven't got pathos in our songs". Well the reason is that most of our songs came out of the dinkie-minnie – the dinkie-minnie was a creative centre for our folk songs and stories, etc. The whole thing is that you were not to be sad, nothing sorrowful should happen at a dinkie. That is why a lot of our folk songs – even if the theme of the song is sad, like in "Linstead Market" – we never sing it sadly. So we must never turn grief inside and let it hurt us. We must let if off.'

Aston Thomas and the great Jah Jerry.

FROM MENTO TO REGGAE

Above – Pamela O'Gorman with Delroy Wilson and Pepe Judah. *Facing* – Garth White in a pensive mood.

Reggae has its roots in the Jamaican folk. In fact, its history is so closely bound up in the Jamaican social and cultural experience that genuine reggae music has remained largely defiant of outside cultural swamping and imitation. Most Jamaicans (and many non-Jamaicans) would concur with Pamela O'Gorman when she says: 'I really do believe that there is something in the so-called myth that Europeans cannot play reggae music. I think they can get the basic things out of it, they can reproduce it to a certain extent. But it is never going to have that touch of authenticity about it.'

The growing popularity of reggae music in recent years obviously opens up the possibility of diluting influences seeping into the art form, but as Pamela O'Gorman points out, this is met by a stronger desire among many reggae artists to maintain the essential integrity of their music. 'People like Toots Hibbert (of the Maytals),' she notes, 'go back to their roots whenever they feel that their music is getting too much European influence, or when they feel that they are performing to a European audience rather than Jamaican. Toots himself goes into seclusion whenever he feels this. He goes back to his mother – who is said to be a Pukkumina shepherdess (i.e. an Afro-religious cult leader) – and he absorbs that whole cultural roots thing again. So he never really gets that far away from the authentic elements of his music.'

There are differences of opinion about the influences that have made their mark on reggae music. Some cultural historians emphasise the Afro-religious basis of the music, while others stress the secular background. But it is widely accepted that Reggae grew directly out of Ska and Rock Steady – that there is a clear line of progression from Ska through Rock Steady to Reggae. This development in contemporary Jamaican popular music started in the 1950's, at a time when Jamaican society was experiencing rapid, and often violent changes. It is marked by a series of changes in musical form and content, partly influenced by non-Jamaican elements, but more strongly rooted in the Afro-Jamaican tradition. This is also the period when Jamaican popular music was beginning to make an impression on the world scene.

Mento

Mento is one of the best-known traditional Jamaican folk forms, and is considered by many people to be the true forerunner of Ska/Rock Steady/Reggae. Dating the origins of Mento is not easy, but Garth White reckons that it probably first appeared around the late 19th century. What is certain, in any case, is that it was largely an entertainment form of music which became one Set of the Quadrille. It contains a mixture of influences – African, European and Latin American – but its overall expression is distinctly Jamaican. Indeed, by the late 1940s and early 1950s, Mento enjoyed immense popularity as *the* national folk dance in Jamaica.

Mento has often been mistaken for the Calypso, a Trinidadian folk form which was also very popular in Jamaica in the 1950s. The two forms are fairly similar, and Mento was certainly influenced by aspects of the Calypso. But the Mento dance – a kind of shuffle step over a small space, with hip-sway and rolling pelvis – was slower and emphasised more the sensual and suggestive aspects of dance, rather than conveying the mainly satirical and political overtones of Calypso. Although Garth White maintains that the Mento also had political content, 'in so far as it dealt with topical subjects and was coming from the poorer sections of the community.'

The significance of Mento in Jamaican popular music, however, is still hotly debated among cultural historians, musicologists, and even musicians. Edward Seaga gives it less weight, compared to the folk idioms associated with religious cult groups and other folk activity, such as Ring Play games. But Louise Bennett argues that there is a definite link between the African heritage, Mento and later forms of Jamaican popular music. For example, such Jamaican standards as 'Come Let Me Hold Your Hand' (which is called the 'Jamaican Welcome Song' in the island), she suggests, are actually Mento songs; and are generally accompanied by folk dances with set steps: 'They have the dipping step which is called the **yanga**, the weak-knee which you still find in Reggae. You find in Reggae a lot of this weak-kneed movement. And this **yanga** step is very prominent in a lot of the Mento.'

Louise Bennett goes on to suggest that Pukkumina, the Afro-Christian religious form, underlies the whole movement of the Mento. This is evidenced in such traditional religious songs as 'Ruggy Ruggy Road,' in which the beat is very much like that of the Ska. What she maps out, then, is an extensive blending of musical and cultural elements which also cut across religious and secular lines. Thus the African **yanga** step, the movement and style of the Mento, rhythmic elements from Pukkumina, etc., all have more or less passed through Ska into contemporary Reggae.

Olive Lewin proposes a rather different genealogy from the one suggested by Louise Bennett. For a start, she stresses the point that the roots of Reggae are to be found in the Jamaican religious tradition and not in Mento – 'because Mento was definitely secular, it is not part of our religious heritage'. She goes on to explain: 'Reggae came out of Revival through Ska. Ska represented a conscious effort to shake off the European influence in Jamaican popular music. So the musicians went to what they knew best, which was Revival. Hence a song like 'Wings of a Dove', which is a straight Revival tune that has been souped-up a little. And if you

Olive Lewin head of folk music for the Prime Minister's office.

go to a Revival Thanksgiving Table (i.e. an Afro-Christian ritual feast), you will find that a lot of the movements there are what Ska came from. Young people used to see these and feel that their grannies were dancing like the Ska. But it was really that their dance (the Ska) was founded on their grannies' movement.'

Ska

'The first man that talked about Ska out here was a man, I don't think they even mention him, Klugie and the Blues Busters, that was the name of his band. And one day he was trying to get the guitars to play something, and him say "make the guitars go Ska! Ska! Ska!" And that's the way the Ska name was born.' – Bunny Lee (leading record producer)

Ska arrived on the scene in the late 1950s. It was the first uniquely Jamaican popular music to gain a wider acceptance. Combining elements of both Mento and Afro-American Rhythm and Blues (and a touch of Jazz), Ska was primarily an instrumental music which was danced to. One enthusiastic commentator in a local newsreel at the time put it thus: 'Jamaica's Ska is the latest popular sound. The rhythm dominates the melody and consequently a driving beat provides an irresistible urge to dance.'

The 'heavy, corporeal rhythm' of the Ska was produced by a unique blending of the R & B 'shuffle rhythm' (i.e. the classic 4/4 driving 'boogie beat'), with a particular guitar pattern of the Mento, and a syncopated bass. Like so many brilliant strokes, the operation here was technically quite simple, though far from obvious. The Jamaican musicians accentuated the 'afterbeat' of the standard 1-2-3-4 / 1-2-3-4 / etc. 'boogie beat' – so that now, as Garth White describes, 'the piano or rhythm guitar emphasised the "and" of one-**and**-two-**and**-three-**and**-four-**and** etc. The drummer meanwhile played the conventional four beats to the bar on the bass drum and the back-beat on the snare.' Not surprisingly, perhaps, the resulting Ska sound did not fall too easily on non-Jamaican ears; and as Garth White goes on to note, it 'led foreign writers and musicians to speak of Ska/Rock Steady/Reggae as R & B and Rock and Roll turned upside down, around and "over on its back".'

Although a lot of emphasis tends to be given to the R & B influence on Ska, by no means was this the only striking feature about the new music. Louise Bennett and Olive Lewin have both noted the carry-over of Revival-Pukkumina movements into Ska dance steps. An example of this is the 'train' movement of the Pukkimina – where the body is bent forward, the arms held out straight, and fists loosely doubled which move backwards and forwards in a pumping movement... Ska dancing has this action. Another feature of the Ska dance, this time originating in the secular folk tradition, has been traced to the 'riding and whipping' movement of the 'Jockey dance' in contemporary Jonkonnu. This step is rather like dance-mime set against a heavy beat.

How, or why did all these musical elements come into play at this particular time in Jamaican popular culture? What triggered the emergence of Ska? The answer to this lies in the influence of the 'sound system' and, especially, the predicament which the sound system operators and their audiences found themselves in by the late 1950s. This topic is covered more fully in the chapter on 'Ranking Sounds', but a few general points are worth making here, to place the development of Ska in its proper social setting.

The sound system, an early forerunner of the mobile discotheque, first appeared just after the Second World War. The sound system operators – who were notable figures on the Jamaican music scene at the time – would play recorded music at house-parties, dances and other popular venues for a fee. They played mainly Rhythm and Blues, Jazz (especially 'danceable' big band material), and some Mento. But their main staple was undoubtedly R & B.

Top – **Fats Domino**. Bottom – **Little Richard**. Facing – Tommy McCook looks foward to Africa.

The more enterprising operators, like the highly successful Clement Dodd (Coxone/Downbeat) and the legendary Duke Reid, would travel to the States to buy the latest R & B records which they would bring back to Jamaica. Success depended on the sound system operator having exclusive control over his material (which was achieved usually by disguising the record's origins or true title), and of course by having a constant supply of the latest and hottest R & B tune.

But the late fifties saw a decline of R & B, as the American record producing companies started to push white-dominated Rock and Roll. This marked a critical turning point for the Jamaican sound system operators. The growing shortage of R & B records meant that they could no longer service the needs of their sound systems and their audiences adequately. Rock and Roll made no big impression on Jamaican audiences, particularly among the followers of sound systems, who preferred the 'rootsier' sound of R & B. And though the handful of Black Rock and Rollers, like Fats Domino and Little Richard, were not ignored, their music did not have the same gutsy impact as R & B.

So the Jamaican sound system men turned to producing their own records. Their success still depended on them coming up with sounds that suited local tastes. Initially, the sound systems made their own 'dubs' by getting local musicians to 'play over' the 'shuffle rhythm'. In other words, the first wave of Jamaican popular music was very close to the R & B variety which they were accustomed to. But this set-up provided the nucleus around which a more indigenous popular music was eventually to evolve – Ska.

The musicians at the centre of this new development came from both Mento and Jazz/R & B backgrounds. Mento had been recorded during the fifties, not on a large scale, but enough to have set a precedent of some kind which could be developed on. This facilitated the Mento musicians' move into the new Ska form, and enhanced their acceptance among local audiences. Artists such as Laurel Aitken, Clue J (Cluet Johnson), Baba Brooks, and Toots Hibbert, to name only a few, helped to keep active specifically Jamaican folk/Mento elements in the popular music.

The musicians who came into Ska from a Jazz background, on the other hand, brought with them a different set of musical ideas and practises. Many of them, like tenor saxophonist Tommy McCook, had attended the renowned Alpha Boys School in West Kingston, where they received formal musical training. Alpha which

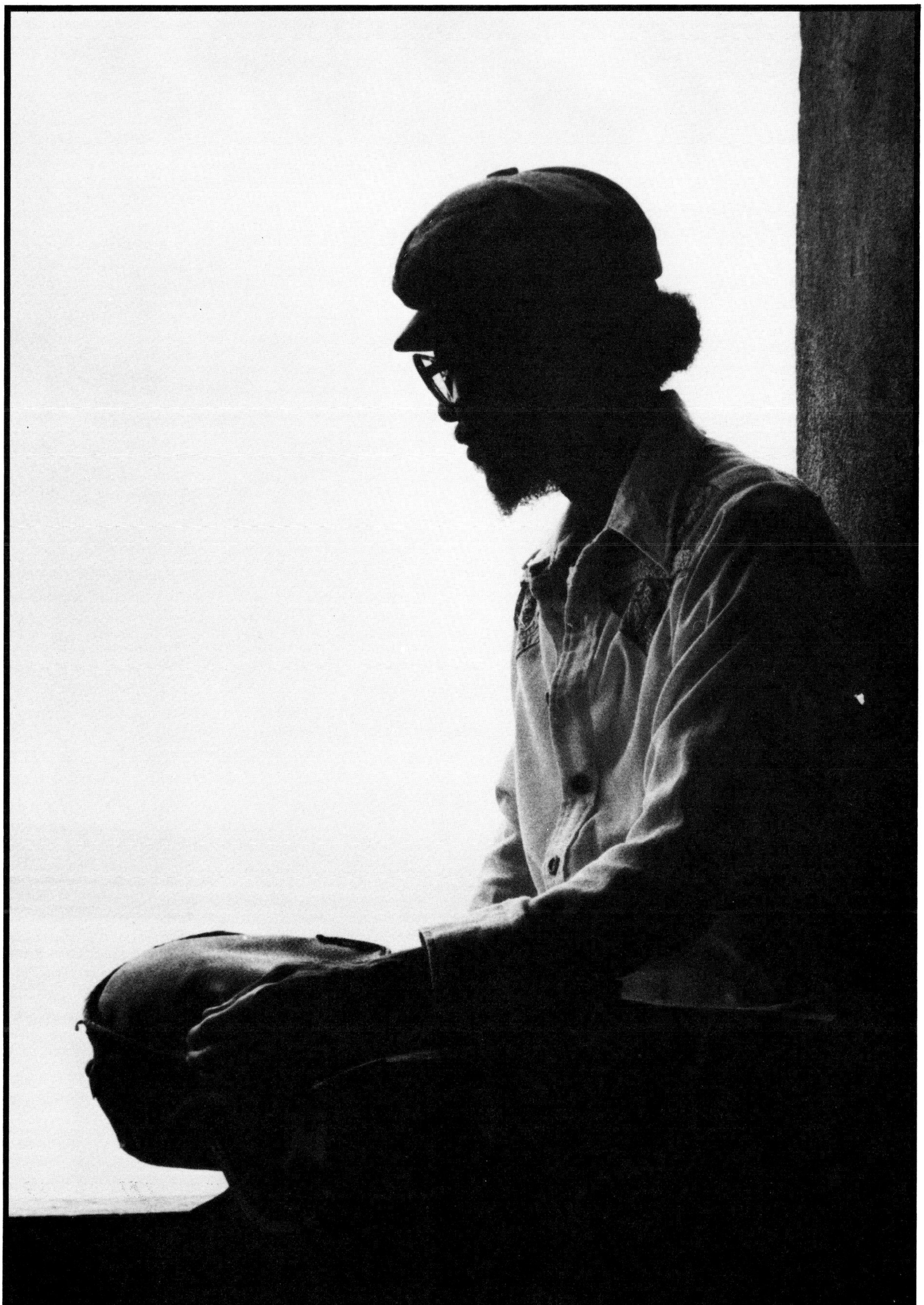

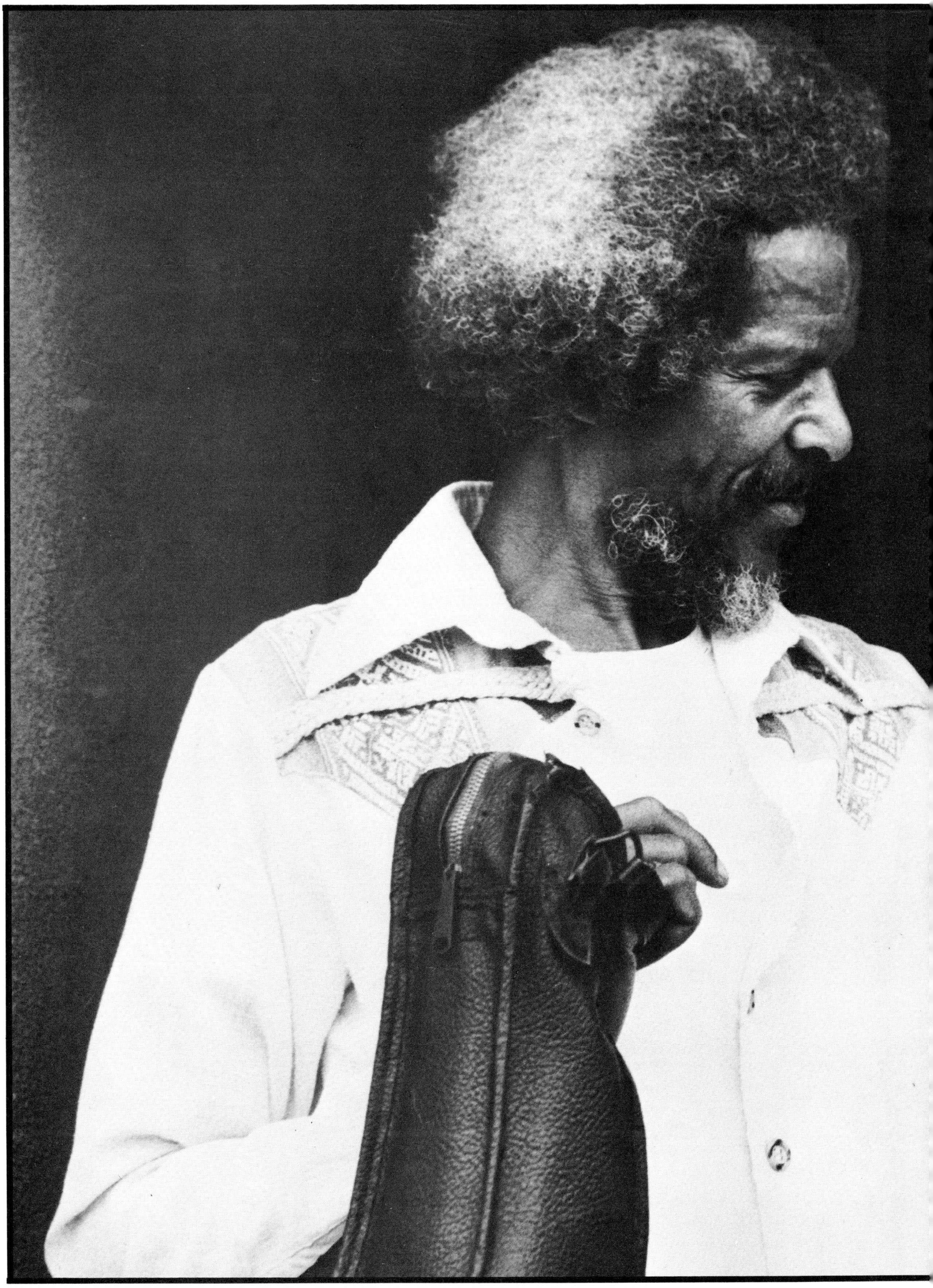

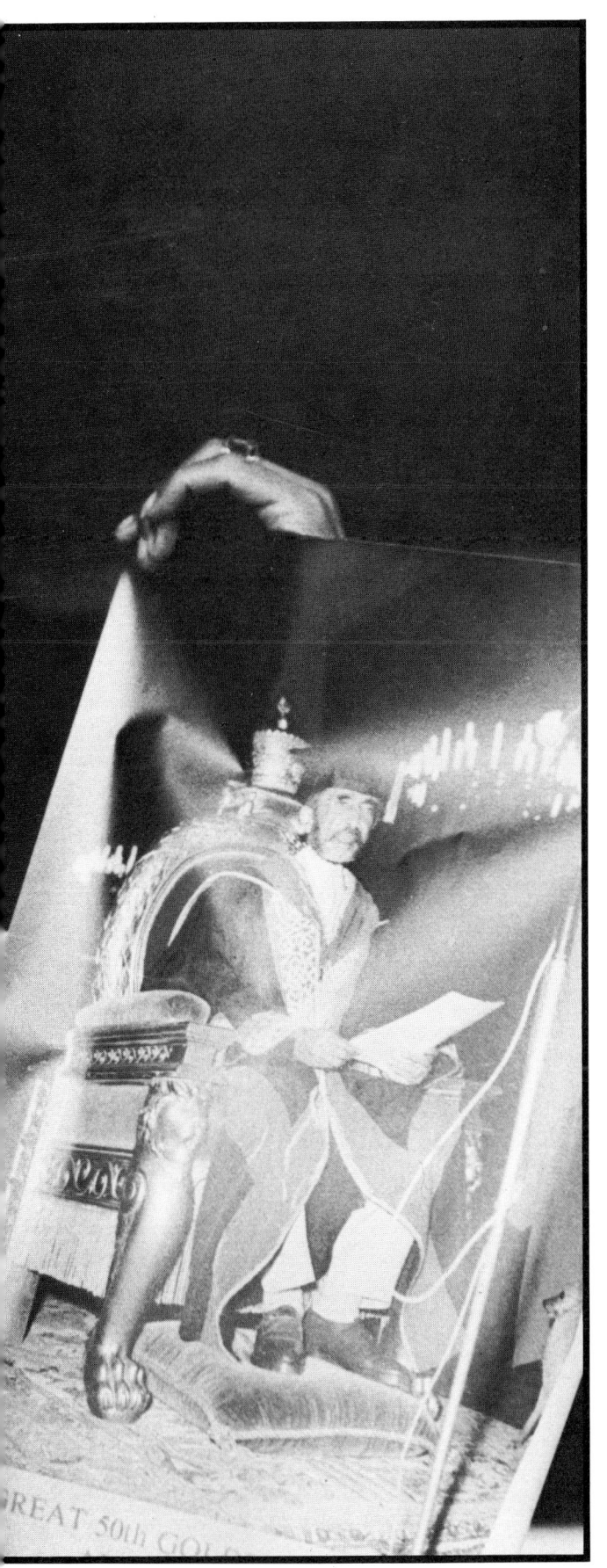

Tommy McCook pays homage to Emperor Haile Selassie.

took in boys from underprivileged backgrounds tended to emphasise the European musical tradition – 'mostly march music, classical, the symphonic side of music,' McCook recalls. 'I became a full member of the Alpha band and we started going out to play at garden parties, functions in the country and other events like that. Quite a few of the internationally known musicians from that era were at Alpha then: Wilton Gaynair, Owen Grey, Roy Harper, Herman Marquis and Joe Harriot.' After leaving school, McCook was soon playing professionally with Derek Deans and Roy Coburn, who had the biggest dance bands in Jamaica at that time.

It was also during this period in the late 1940s, that Rasta music was beginning to gain momentum, under the guiding influence of the legendary master drummer Count Ossie, whose own roots stemmed from the Buru tradition. But this development remained largely independent of the more popular musical trends during the period. The Rastas themselves were constantly harassed by the authorities, which only hardened the common stereotype of them as social and cultural outcasts. 'They had to hide to play their music,' recalls Tommy McCook, 'because the police would come to mash them up. At times they chopped up the drums and beat up some of the players. So the Rastas had to go further back to the hills, so it would be harder for the police to get at them.'

But despite these pressures, there were important exchanges happening between certain non-Rasta musicians and Rastas, which influenced the creative development of both musical genres. McCook recalls his first encounter with Rastafarian music back in the late forties: 'I used to go to Count Ossie's camp and listen to drumming. And then they would invite me to come and blow with them. On certain

The beautiful Jah Jerry plays his guitar in his back yard.

evenings when I was free I would go and sit with them – what we would call "have a grounation". The drums would start playing and you would come in and play whatever song you felt like playing – for you were all alone on your own instrument. There wasn't any guitar or piano or bass. It was just drums keeping time. So whatever song you chose to play, you had to remember everything in that song to make it sound right. Then I chanted with the singing of the Rasta songs, played in between the Rasta psalms. It was a lovely experience. I went back on many occasions.'

Then in 1954, McCook left for Nassau in the Bahamas, to join a dance band there. During this period he was playing late forties big band jazz tunes like Count Basie's 'Flying Home' and Duke Ellington's 'Sophisticated Lady'. 'I came back to Jamaica in 1960 for a vacation – I liked the vibes that were then in Jamaica. I heard the Ska for the first time and the "boogie" on the local radio. I had heard one or two records while I was in Nassau, but it didn't really reach me then.' McCook returned to Nassau to fulfill his contract, but by now he had decided that he would return home to Jamaica, which he did in 1962.

'When I came back, Don Drummond was the man on the scene; he had this hit tune out at the time, called "Schooling the Duke". I listened to the music but I was playing jazz at the time, and Louis Jordan music. We had this little jazz club called the Village Gate up in Vineyards Town. While I was there Coxsone [Dodd] came and asked me if I would do some local recordings for him. I never really thought about it, as I was really concentrating on the jazz scene. He came to me again in '63 and I decided that I would give it a try. So I got involved in the Ska. I did a couple of instrumentals for Coxsone – the first one was called "Road Block", and a tune called "Exodus", which was my first local Ska recording.'

In the same year, Tommy McCook was instrumental in forming one of the most important bands in the history of Jamaican music – The Skatalites. The group included some of Jamaica's most talented jazz musicians around at the time: Don Drummond (trombone), Roland Alphonso (tenor saxophone), Johnny Moore (trumpet), Lester Stirling (alto saxophone), Lloyd Brevette (bass), Lloyd Knibbs (drums), Jah Gerry (guitar), who was mainly a Rhythm and Blues musician, and Jackie Mittoo (piano).

The group originally had been working together as a studio-based recording outfit; they were not engaged in live concerts. McCook remembers how people kept asking him who played various tunes they heard on the records. Realising the implications of this public interest in their recordings, he suggested to the others that they form a proper band to do live performances. They were reluctant at first, but eventually agreed if McCook would lead it. 'I was already in a group at the time, but I thought it over and finally left the band I was in, and we formed the Skatalites. By this time we were doing more recordings together. I became a sort of featured soloist on the records. They would want a horn to solo in between the singing. When the singer breaks, I would take a few bars of the music and improvise, then turn it back to the singer. I did a few of these and it was well-liked. When the people started hearing the sound, now, they started to flock the scene.' In a very short time, the Skatalites came to represent Ska at its zenith.

Given their rich musical backgrounds, it was a unique kind of chemistry that enabled the Skatalites to create the indigenous Ska music in the way that they did. Garth White interprets this as an example of the 'cross-fertilisation and interweaving of music' that you find in Jamaican culture. And he sees it as a positive process of creativity: 'The Skatalites had the jazz background and the Rasta background, and they combined all this in the Ska. So you would hear themes from the old traditional culture in their music, up-dated versions of Rhythm and Blues, jazz standards, and they would even re-work tunes from the movies. They were highly skilled musicians and very good improvisers.

'The line-up included Don Drummond. He really was fantastic, both as a composer and as an instrumentalist. He knew no boundaries. He would take the simplest Ska tune and make it into a gem. This was in the face of official indifference – which is to say that the kind of music that the Skatalites were playing was seen by the establishment as "bongo" music. Yet despite this, the musicians kept on. They were superb instrumentalists, their output was phenomenal.'

Tommy McCook's comments about Don Drummond aptly bear out Garth White's enthusiasm: 'Don came on the scene initially about '52. He became very popular and was playing with good bands at the time. He was a member of the band that backed Sarah Vaughan (the leading Afro-American jazz singer) when she came to Jamaica and performed, at the Glass Bucket club. She heard him for the first time and told the Jamaican public that she figured that he was rated in the first five in the world. From then on Don lived up to what Sarah said – he was even thought of at one time as being the best in the world. His tone on the trombone, his approach, everything was so perfect. I considered him a genius on his instrument. Even other players of the instrument expressed this, and they should know.'

Don Drummond was both a musical genius and a tragic hero of Jamaican music. He was completely devoted to his music and strove for excellence. But his mind was in torment, and this is what got the better of him in the end. The Skatalites broke up in late 1965, largely because of this and other personal problems within the group. They had been branded, needless to say, unfairly by certain sections of the Jamaican public as 'the bad boys from Alpha'; and this contributed to some extent to the group not being given the promotional boost that they deserved. Nevertheless what the Skatalites achieved during their brief reign as the leading innovative

Right – The Hon. Edward Seaga with his wife, Lady Bustamante, and his son, with bodyguards, Trinity and Company behind him at a Sunday Heritage service. Facing – Jackie Edwards.

band, had a resounding and lasting effect on the development of Jamaican popular music.

Jamaican Independence in 1962 saw a shift in attitude towards the indigenous music. The new government discouraged the importation of foreign music and made a concentrated effort to promote Jamaican music. For the first time, Jamaica's musical culture became a national asset. Edward Seaga, and active promoter of the music at that time, tried to introduce Ska to the North American public, by sending a troupe of musicians and dancers to the 1964 New York World's Fair. The purpose of this exercise was clearly to promote a new Jamaican national image abroad. To a large extent it succeeded. It would only be a matter of a few years before Jamaica's music industry, like its bauxite counterpart, would be bucking against the commercial market establishments of the world.

But during this same period, Jamaican society itself went through a major social upheaval. The post-independence 'honeymoon' ended rather abruptly. Indeed, like the post-emancipation period a century earlier, the post-independence years spawned a wave of social unrest among the poor and there was mounting violence of one kind or another. It was a period marked (and marred) by pervasive tension and conflict in Jamaica, where criminal and political violence became an everyday occurrence. Needless to say, this was a legacy of slavery and colonisation, where fear and terror had been an integral feature of domination and social control in the island. It was an expression of something deeply embedded in the Jamaican experience. And it is also what, to use Pamela O'Gorman's words, 'has given a kind of edge to the popular music.'

There is a long tradition in Jamaican music of providing commentary on social and political issues. It is very often couched in religious imagery and satire in earlier music, especially during slavery. But the inception of Rastafari in the late 1930's saw a much stronger use of protest lyrics. Inspired by the teachings of Marcus Mosiah Garvey (see chapter 4), Rasta music openly attacked the *status quo* and asserted Black dignity and consciousness. Ska continued this musical tradition of protest and social commentary, although not in such a total sense as Rastafari. Much of Ska was still essentially entertainment dance music. Nevertheless, the fact that most of the artists came out of the ghetto experience, did mean that some popular songs dealt with burning issues like poverty, oppression, unemployment and so on.

Ska was on the wane by the mid-1960's. 'According to one producer,' recalls Tommy McCook, 'Duke Reid [the celebrated sound system operator] said that his fans were getting tired of dancing to the Ska all night. It was too fast and they weren't as young as they used to be. So they asked him if he could slow down the music and give them a different beat other than the Ska. This is how we got to Rock Steady – which is really a Ska but in a slower form.'

Rock Steady

Rock Steady was a more relaxed music, involving less exertion for the dancers. The instrumental phrasing of melodies was more extended. The off-beat was accentuated even further, with the drummer now dropping in between the 2nd and 4th beats, in a style that became known as 'the one drop'. The bass was rhythmically more developed in the Rock Steady, although it was still built largely on a repetitive motif. The bass line was also more melodic in character, and it was used in a call-and-response to the vocal line. The slowing of tempo – or, 'cutting the rhythm in half' – in Rock Steady offered more scope for singers to work within, which resulted in the vocal element becoming more prominent than before. However, the overpowering rhythmic drive of the amplified bass – the characteristic 'booming bass' – has led some commentators to regard Rock Steady as essentially dance music.

The Rock Steady period ushered in a new wave of outstanding vocalists. Tommy McCook still ranks Alton Ellis as 'the giant of that era. He dug into the beat more than any other artist and created hits after hits. His music stands up even today in the midst of Reggae.' Other big names of the day included Derrick Morgan, Ken Boothe, Justin Hinds, the young Jimmy Cliff, Desmond Dekker, Jackie Edwards, Delroy Wilson (in a duo with Joe Higgs) and many others. The vocal style of these singers varied widely. Some imitated Blues and R & B styles, others were largely Ska-orientated, while still others were more grounded in the Rock Steady idiom. This variety reflected the range of popular black music which the public was hearing at the time.

For example, Nat 'King' Cole, the brilliant Afro-American jazz pianist with the soft velvety singing voice, was very popular in Jamaica in the fifties and sixties. He represented 'The Man With The Golden Voice', who sang of Love and Romance. Many young singers in Jamaica who sang at talent contests, held on Saturday mornings at the Carib and Regal cinemas, and on radio shows like Vere John's Talent Hour, tried to imitate the great Nat 'King' Cole or another favourite, Billy Ekstine.

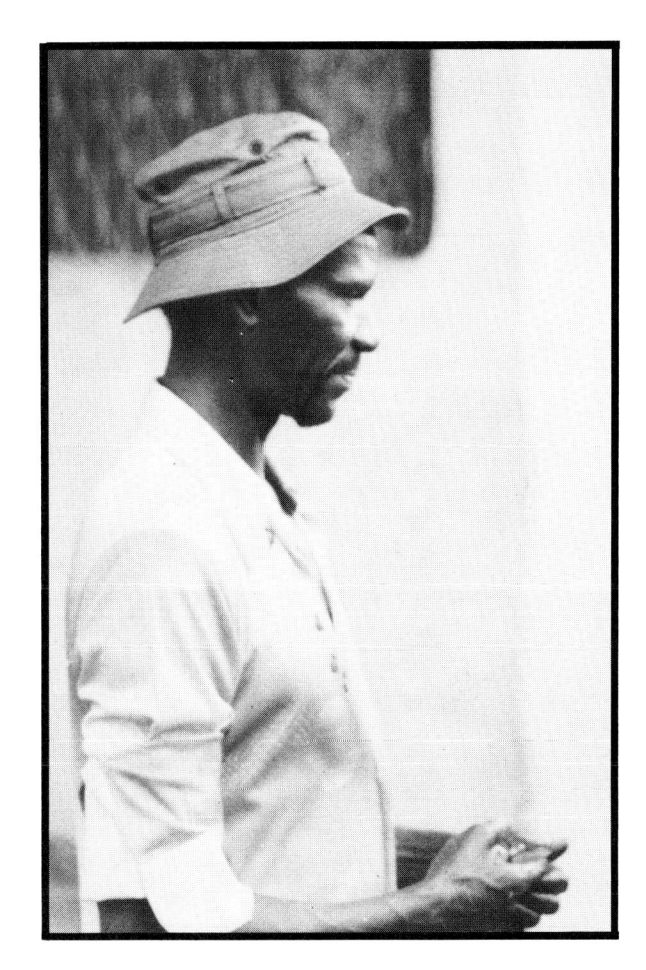

'Long ago they used to call me Mr Soft,' recalls Jackie Edwards, a romantic lyricist and one of the pioneers of Jamaican popular music. 'I used to like Nat 'King' Cole and I said to myself, "I'm going to sound like that man." I tried it and it worked. But after a while I decided to switch off and create my own style. But even nowadays, if I want to I can sound just like Nat Cole.'

Contemporary R & B (i.e. 'Soul') was also regularly played on the local radio during this period. 'Soul' was largely concerned with themes of love and romance; and those Jamaican vocalists who took it up tended also to emulate the Afro-American style of voicing. The legendary Delroy Wilson readily admits his own interest in the genre: 'Well, to be frank, I used to listen to Marvin Gaye, Stevie Wonder, Lou Rawls. So listening to them, I tried to put everything together and form my own kind of style of singing.'

Below – **Stevie Wonder**. Facing – **Jimmy Cliff** in a pensive mood.

Whatever their particular style, all of these singers worked with or were produced by the top sound systems of the period. The sound system was alive and well – providing an outlet for the whole range of local musical talent that was bursting with creative energy, and providing the kind of music that the more discerning audience wanted to hear. The main staple was naturally Rock Steady. This was the music that not only offered entertainment, but also drew attention to social realities in more explicit terms. In this respect, Rock Steady contrasted sharply with the bulk of 'Soul' being played at the time; and its lyrics contained more bite or 'dread' than Ska. However, it would be incorrect to say that Rock Steady was 'conscious music' as such, but rather that social consciousness became one of the major themes in the Rock Steady repertoire.

'Even from the days of Ska,' states Garth White, 'you had tunes dealing with topical events, social and political questions. But it was not as widespread as it became in the pressure period of the late 1960s, when social conditions came to be rendered more explicitly in the lyrics. For example, in Delroy Wilson's 'Conquer Me', Bob Marley and the Wailers' 'Hipocrite' and 'Nice Time', and tunes by The Heptones, The Paragons, Bob Andy, The Melodians and others.'

The 'pressure period' that Garth White refers to covers the height of tension and conflict in the island, which had gathered momentum by about 1965-6. Despite independence and a new national government, nothing radically had changed in the society. This resulted in a deepening antagonism between the 'haves' and 'have-nots', which manifested itself in violent confrontation and fierce resentment coming from below. Gangsterism escalated at an alarming rate: robberies, stabbings, lootings and shootings became everyday occurrences. And to make matters worse, the courts handed down extremely harsh sentences, in an attempt to suppress the upsurge of anti-establishment feelings, particularly among the younger generation.

This was the era of the Rude Boys, the 'rough and tough' youths who set out to challenge the *status quo* head-on. The Rudies epitomised rebellion at its starkest – brandishing machetes and other cutting implements, toting guns, carrying explosives on certain occasions. And they used these weapons – though most often on fellow blacks! Rude Boy culture absorbed the Hollywood gangster image and made it into a

58

nervous kind of reality. Johnny-Too-Bad had come to life.

Dandy Livingstone's 'We Are Rude' extolled the virtues of the Rudies, in response to Prince Buster's controversial attack on them in 'Judge Dread'. Prince Buster's eponymous (Black) judge hands out sentences of 100 years or more, pretty much at the blink of an eyelid. But Dandy Livingstone's rallying-cry promises to stand up to 'Judge "100 Years" Dread', even if he hands them out sentences of a thousand years! The Rude Boy phenomenon was sufficiently serious enough for quite a few popular songs at the time to express an opinion on the matter, their titles alone convey a sense of the anxiety and passion surrounding the affair – 'Tougher Than Tough', 'Dreader Than Dread', 'Rudies Don't Fear', 'Cool Down Your Temper', '007', 'Pressure Drop', etc.

Many Rude Boys subsequently grew 'dreadlocks' and became Rastas, which only intensified the criminal image of the Rastafarian movement. The Rastafarians were already viewed by the wider society as social outcasts, which was aided by the Rastas self-imposed isolation from mainstream (Babylonian) social life. But now, with the inclusion of the notorious Rude Boys, they were branded as outlaws associated with ganja (marijuana) dealing, gun-running and other 'illegal' activity.

Delroy Wilson.

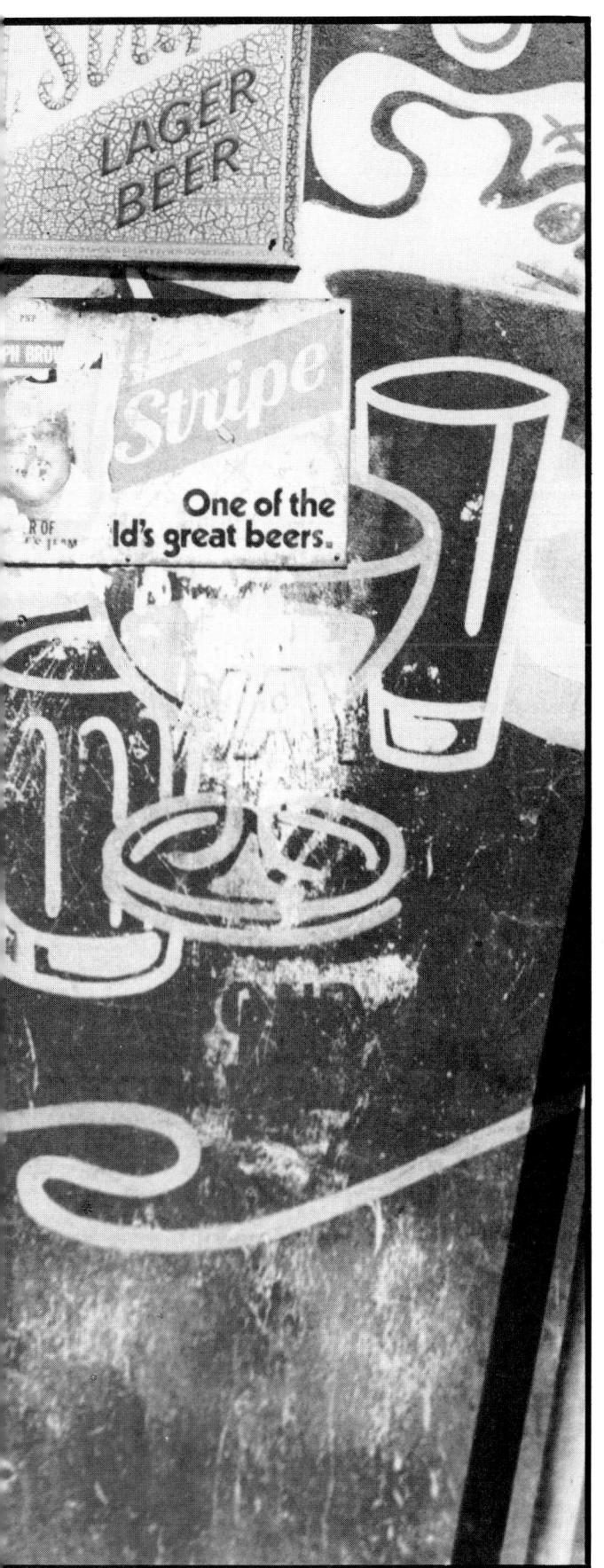

Reggae

The Rock Steady period did not last for very long, although the social and historical conditions out of which it grew remained. Around 1968-9 a new sound came on the scene – it was called Reggae. This represents the latest stage in the development of Jamaican popular music. The origin of the word, 'Reggae', remains a bit of an enigma, however, although not surprisingly, more than one person claims to be its originator or to know who or where it originated from. According to Bunny Lee, whose information is as good as anybody's, the word came about during a recording session when one of the musicians exclaimed: 'Make the organ go Reggae! Reggae! Reggae!' But Toots and the Maytals' 'Do The Reggay', which Toots Hibbert wrote, is evidently the first time the word was used in a recording. Beyond that, nothing is certain.

Reggae combines Ska and Rock Steady with added elements and techniques of its own. This is highlighted in Garth White's description of the basic structure of the music: 'A half-note is added to the classic "after-beat" of the Ska/Rock Steady, which gives one-**anda**-two-**anda**-three-**anda**-four-**anda** etc.' The drummer drops in between the beats as before, only now in a style that produces 'a more "sinuous" and less "jumpy" rhythm.' In addition, 'a Ska or Mento piano or organ may well be added to a Rock Steady bass, or drum with a Mento guitar "filler" and a developed melodic line ... and you have Reggae.'

Reggae has links with both the religious and the secular tradition in Jamaican culture. Olive Lewin pointed out earlier on the strong connection that Reggae has with Revival-Pukkumina, the Afro-Christian religion, via Ska. Then there is the link with the secular Mento, both in terms of instrumentation (i.e. the Mento guitar 'filler'), and in terms of dance movement, the weak-kneed or African **yanga** step which Louise Bennett drew our attention to. Added to all these Afro-Jamaican elements, we have the Afro-American Jazz/R & B influence via Ska/Rock Steady. Reggae is a global synthesis of black musical culture.

Reggae has strong links with other Afro-Jamaican traditions as well. For example, the Prince Buster-Dandy Livingstone 'Rude Boys' exchange is in many respects an extension of the Buru. The Buru tradition, if you recall, utilised songs of derision and lyrical jibes to highlight the moral state of the community. Reggae artists conduct similar kinds of 'debates' in their music. It is a particularly strong feature in Rasta-Reggae, where the lyrics are heavily loaded with moral and social commentary as well as apocalyptic warnings.

The use of protest lyrics and social commentary in Jamaican popular music evolved gradually during the Ska and Rock Steady periods, and reached even greater heights in the present Reggae. The strongest influence on this development has undoubtedly been Rastafarian religion (see chapter 4) whose philosophy and vocabulary have been incorporated into Reggae songs. Bob Marley and the Wailers were the most popular (and commercially successful) exponents of this tradition, spreading the Message in terms which were intelligible to wider audiences.

This populist aspect of Reggae has helped to keep the music firmly entrenched in the black ghetto experience. It is true that many songs take in more universal themes and messages, but the core impulse nevertheless remains rooted in the Afro-Jamaican experience. But the populist impulse in Reggae has also made the music vulnerable to political exploitation. This was revealed most strikingly during Jamaica's General Election in 1972. The People's National Party (P.N.P.), under the leadership of Michael Manley, used Reggae music to a very large extent in its pre-election campaign, especially protest songs that captured the imagination of the population. All this was in keeping with

Bunny Lee (centre) and Jackie Edwards rapping Bunny back yard.

Manley's populist approach to Jamaican politics.

'Many of his speeches,' recounts Pamela O'Gorman, 'were recorded to a background of Reggae music, which had the effect of heightening the whole temperature of the performance you might say.' Delroy Wilson's song, 'Better Must Come', became the P.N.P.'s anthem; and many Reggae artists joined the Party entourage which toured the island in a 'politics-cum-music package'. Michael Manley and the P.N.P. won a landslide victory.

The approach was repeated during the 1976 elections. But by this time, Michael Manley had established himself as a charismatic leader of 'the people' and a spokesman for the 'Third World'. He had also acquired the Biblical name, 'Joshua', which appealed to the religious and spiritual aspects of Jamaican culture. The P.N.P. also tried to use Reggae to popularise certain programmes, such as adult education, national unity, and support for the party.

'I think to a certain extent this caught on,' says Pamela O'Gorman, 'but not altogether, because the musicians themselves rebelled against being used for what they termed "political ends". It's very interesting that for Reggae musicians in Jamaica, if they feel that a cause is just, they will support it. But even a couple of years after Michael Manley came to power, a song came out called "No Joshua No" (by Max Romeo, a former member of the P.N.P. Bandwagon), which warned Mr Manley that certain things he was doing were not approved of.'

During this period political violence had intensified in the island. Political gang war erupted, guns were sold in exchange for ganja (marijuana), thousands of people were killed. A party of ghetto leaders came to London where Bob Marley was residing, after himself being shot, and asked him to return to Jamaica and appeal for peace. The result was the Peace Concert held in Kingston in 1978. Marley made an ecstatic appeal for peace in the island, and got the two leaders of the main political parties – Michael Manley and Edward Seaga – to come together. Hence Marley's endearing tune, 'Jammin'.

Michael Manley, who lost the 1980 election to Edward Seaga's Jamaica Labour Party (J.L.P.), recently recalled the experience: 'Well, I think that that was an important thing. It was an evidence of Marley's concern, concern for the effect just on people of political violence. And it obviously was an evidence of his extraordinary, almost charismatic influence in Jamaican life that he could make it happen.'

Pamela O'Gorman's concluding remarks strongly emphasise the point that Reggae music, despite its vulnerability to political (and commercial) exploitation, will retain its vital function within the Afro-Jamaican experience:

'I'm sure Reggae will continue to be a revolutionary music. No matter how well a political party does. And of course there are great hopes in Jamaica at the moment, that changes will take place. But I think that the problems in Jamaica are so enormous, that I can't see them being resolved overnight or very quickly. And so long as there is injustice in the society – in the sense that one part of the society is living at the expense of another part – you are going to have this tremendous awareness of social inequality, and a tension in the society that is going to give birth to the kind of songs that you get in Reggae.'

Sir Lord Comic and Bobby Aitken pay homage to Alton Ellis.

RANKING SOUNDS

Charlie Parker.

Before the arrival of the 'sound systems' in the early 1950s, popular entertainment music in Jamaica was largely provided by dance bands. These bands played the swinging post-Second World War sounds of Count Basie and Duke Ellington, and the more 'progressive' early-Bop jazz of Charlie Parker and Dizzy Gillespie. The presence of Afro-American jazz was quite substantial during this period in Jamaica's musical history.

As the dance bands faded out of prominence, they were replaced by the sound systems. Sound systems were early forms of mobile discotheques; they provided recorded music at dances, house- and lawn-parties and other such occasions. Initially, the sound systems played mainly Rhythm and Blues – Fats Domino, Bill Doggett and Louis Jordan were big favourites with Jamaican audiences. The men who ran the sound systems supplied their own records, and they conducted their business in a truly entrepreneurial style. Those who could afford it, travelled to the States in order to buy the latest R & B hits. Another source came from American sailors who would bring records and 'swap them for rum'. Still another source was Jamaican farm-workers who migrated to the Southern States, and returned with records to sell.

Once in their hands, the sound system men would immediately scratch the label off the records, so that nobody would know the origin or true title of the tunes – these records came to be known as 'blanks'. Even the operators themselves would forget the original title of the tunes they had purchased, especially after giving the records personal titles of their own. This practice more or less ensured the sound system man's 'exclusive rights' or control over a particularly popular tune.

The men who ran the sound systems attracted a large following, and each system had its own following. There was a great deal of rivalry between systems, and feuds often broke out between supporters of rival systems. However, the sound system men established their reputation and attracted a following on the basis not only of the particular music they played, but also on the capabilities of the sound equipment they had. Each system was noted for its particular quality of sound; but a 'heavy' bass was almost always a sure avenue to success. The top sound systems around at the time included Duke Reid (who named his system Treasure

The Legendary Duke Reid

Island), Clement 'Coxsone' Dodd (Downbeat), Prince Buster, Tom (the Great Sebastian), Count Nick and many others. The satirical use of 'titles' in their names connects the sound system men, in certain respects, to the folk tradition – a Jonkonnu without the masks (or with a different kind of mask) would be an appropriate analogy, but the Buru man is there too.

Unlike dance bands, the sound system attracted a working class following. 'What it did,' says Garth White, 'was to provide the Black people with a new means of communication, one that was much more powerful than anything that they had in the past.' Garth White emphasises the point that the sound system did more to shape and popularise Jamaican popular music, than another other contemporary medium such as radio, night clubs or stage shows.

By the late 1950s, R & B records became less available, because of the shift in the American record companies towards white Rock and Roll. Faced with this apparent set-back, the sound system men decided that they would produce their own music, aimed specifically at the local audience. At first, they came up with music that was very similar to the Rhythm and Blues that they were accustomed to. But within a short period of time, they were promoting a new indigenous sound – Ska. The local musicians who previously were playing jazz in dance bands, now became the principle exponents of the new music of Jamaica. The sound system men thus became the first indigenous record producers. But as Garth White points out, they had not really departed very much from their original objectives: 'They decided to record music more suited to local tastes for their own purposes – to service their sound. It was primarily to service their own sound system. I don't think they had in mind the large scale thing of today.'

'He was ever great,' – Mrs Duke Reid

Duke Reid had served in the police force for ten years, before resigning his job to join his wife in her liquor store business. Mrs Reid vividly recalls how 'he eventually got a little sound system at the time and some box, and he started to play about four hours each day. And you know you have a lot of people around, they like the sound and they like the records. So he decided to go all out in the sound system. And so he bought some boxes [i.e. huge speakers]. The first time he played was at Drummond Street, matinee dance. People loved the music and they loved the sound and he was a very nice man.' Mrs Reid remembers how Duke's enthusiastic followers would wait excitedly for his arrival ahd how they would 'actually lift him out of his car' like a king. The whole hall would pack up when Duke came. 'And after his sound is set up and he is about to play, everybody would start to clap and really make a lotta noise. They would say, "Duke, Duke is on now!" He's the king of the sound.'

Mrs Reid remembers Duke having six big speaker boxes, 'and his sound always had good bass, a powerful bass. And that would draw a lot of people. He never failed in any of his music... he was always on top of all the other sounds.' One of the big crowd-pulling events was when rival systems challenged each other to contests, to see who had the Number One sound. Apparently, Duke always won hands down. On one occasion he beat two of his arch rivals after playing his theme tune, 'My Mother's Eyes'. Mrs Reid remembers the audience lifting Duke up and crowning him 'Duke the Trojan'.

From his days in the police force, Duke Reid always carried a gun, 'as protection,' says Mrs Reid, continuing, 'No, he wasn't afraid of anybody. He's a very stern person. He's a

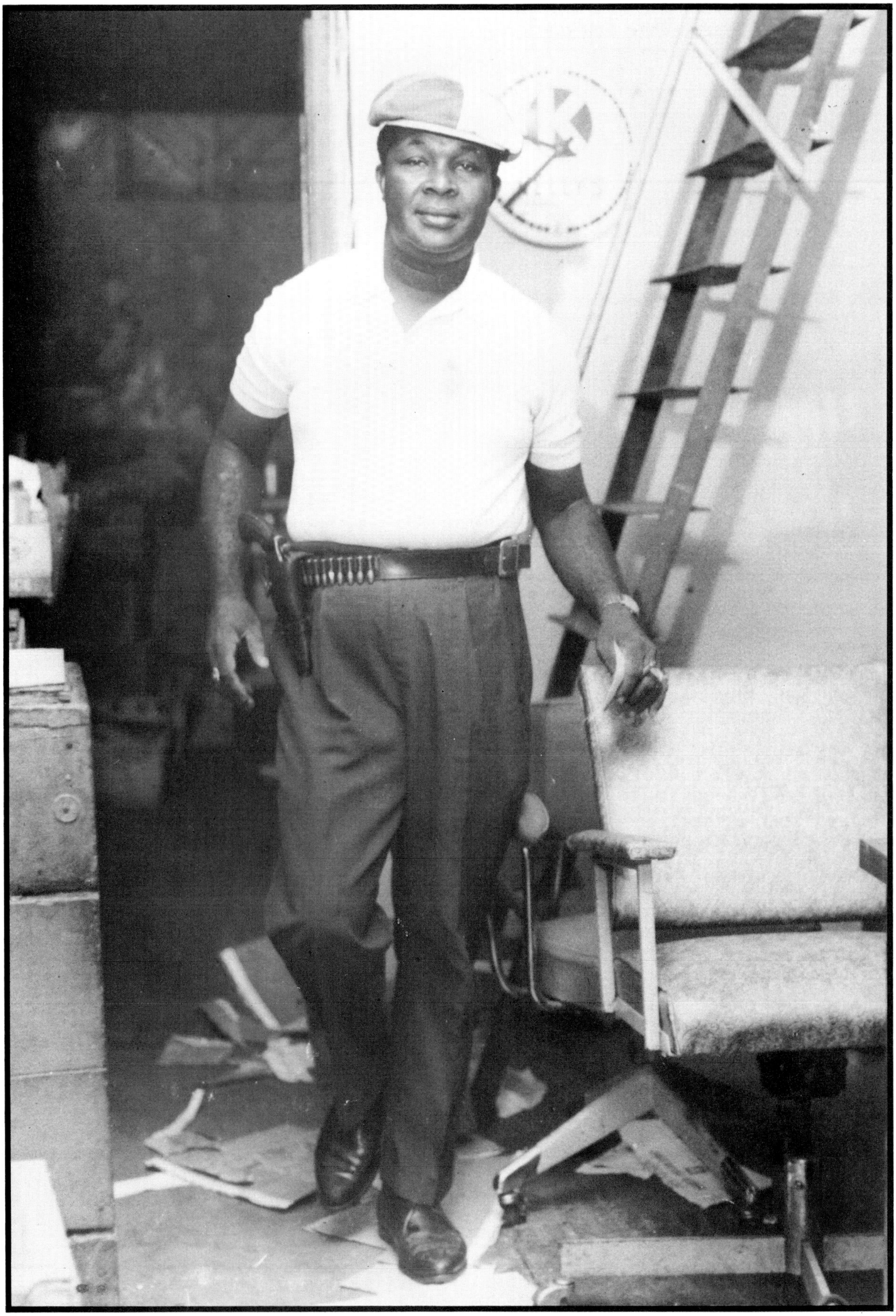

Opposite – The great Duke Reid with his Colt ·45. The man who slowed the Ska to Rocksteady. Right – Mrs Duke Reid and Pampadour reminiscing about the great Duke Reid.

principled type of person. He makes a lot of jokes, but when it comes to serious, he's very serious.' Mr Pampadour, Duke Reid's long-time dance hall partner, recalls that 'Sometimes they used to try to tape off his tune, which sometimes call contention. Other sound men try to tape off his tune, like the first local tune he recorded, an instrumental called "Dukie's Cookie".'

Duke Reid was also an astute businessman. He operated two separate sound systems, which he designated as the 'Number One' sound and the 'Number Two' sound. 'The Number One sound was a heavier set,' explains Pampadour, 'a bigger set. It carried more top tunes. If you wanted the Number One, you had to pay more to hire it. You had to be a regular promoter to get it because Duke didn't want the Number One sound to flop. So if he doesn't know if you can draw a crowd, you can't get the Number One sound.'

The competition was so intense between rival sounds that each was waiting for the opportunity to 'flop' the other – i.e. pull the crowd away from one's rival into one's own venue, which would be happening at the same time and perhaps only down the road. The worst thing that could happen to a sound was if word got round that so-and-so 'flop' him last night. 'So therefore,' says Pampadour, 'you have to be popular to get the Number One sound. The promoters have to be popular because they have to get the crowd.' To ensure himself, Duke Reid always played the Number One set himself. He did not DJ, however, that was left to one of his six aides. His popularity as the top sound system man was at a peak in 1956.

'After he finished with the sound,' says Mrs Reid, 'he decided to build his own studio (Treasure Isle) and do his own recordings. That was in the early 1960s.' Derek Morgan was the first artist he recorded. This was followed by innumerable hits, including one called 'Yard Broom'; 'Twelve Minutes To Go', which was played by the Skatalites; Justin Hinds' classic, 'Carry Go Bring Come'; and U-Roy's witty sing-talk tunes, 'Wake the Town and Tell the People' and 'This Station is the Real Station'. In 1974, while terminally ill, Duke Reid sold Treasure Isle, its equipment and all his master tapes, to Sonia Pottinger, one of the few women Reggae producers working in Jamaica today.

'I would say he has contributed a lot to the music,' says Tommy McCook, 'because he was interested in the changes; he never fought the changes, and he always tried to please the people. Duke Reid and Coxsone Dodd are the two main people for exposing the talent that Jamaica has produced. Well it is said that Coxsone is really the leading producer. He has done more recordings than any other producer. And he has the best that Jamaica has produced on records. A lot of the new producers in Jamaica today have to give Coxsone Downbeat credit, because more than once they have used his ridims. I understand that Coxsone has no less than about two thousand tapes that he hasn't listened back to, that he hasn't heard since he recorded them...'

The Art of Toasting

*'I remember the first night in the new Carnival Hall, along 87, North Street. I used there words to sell our local recordings: "French Canadian home-cooked musical biscuit," And folks dig it, you know, and so I found myself preparing something new to say to the folks. I developed jives like: "I'm hard to catch, I'm hard to hold." I found that people go **crazy**, so you know I keep digging, digging, I came up with "Live the life you love and love the life you live", "Whether you be young or old, you just got to let the good time roll, my friend!" I keep rolling in the audience, and our local recording was getting a break. Eventually, I found that I could play all Jamaican recordings, strictly no foreign recordings, strictly Jamaican. Because I had a live jive to sell it, you know. I don't really call myself a D.J. I call myself an off-the-record disciple, that is how I look at myself.' – Count Machouki*

Count Machouki originated the art of 'toasting'. What he did was to elevate the status of the sound system D.J. – from a person who merely puts the records on, to a sage-like hero placed at the centre of the live musical experience. 'In my time,' he says, 'a D.J. was a man who was responsible for conduct and behaviour, and what goes on inside the dance hall. And we used the music as a message to control the hearts and minds of the people, and utter – we didn't realise then that *word is power*, and the words that we used really could control the people.'

In the sound system days, the D.J. was in personal contact with his audience. 'We could actually talk to the audience,' says Count Machouki, 'and everybody was happy, y'know. We didn't have to really be singing on the records to keep everybody happy. We just make utterances before a record, introduce the artists, give an idea of the message that the artist is going to give you. And sometimes when we listen to the record and find that music is wanting, we would inter-serve something like "Get on the ball..." and cover that weakness in the record. It was live jive and it really made people feel happy. It was our sole intention to sell happiness to our own Jamaicans. In these days it has become more commercialised, really.'

Sir Lord Comic, a protege of Count Machouki, adds the point that during the early period (and still today, but not in such large quantities), people would go to dances just to see them perform live. 'But in these days,' he adds regretfully, 'the guys don't deal with the D.J. as such.'

'I came into this business with one intention,' says Count Machouki, 'that when the radio station needed a D.J., they could look in the sound fields and find guys who have the ability to really get on to the people. Because the guys who play the sounds have that mass appeal – we have the roots connection, we can at least

Opposite – **Count Machouki:**
*"Live the life you love
Love the life you live.
Whether you be young or old
You just gotta let the good time roll, my friend."*
Left – Sir Lord Comic outside Tip Top records down town Kingston.

communicate with each and everyone.'

Like other artists who struggle to retain their integrity, Count Machouki more or less withdrew from the scene: 'Somewhere along the way, the financial returns didn't really suit me. So I just stay on the fence and keep looking in. That's why it's so hard for them to catch me – they come along but the can't get at me, because I keep looking in. I don't like getting involved unless I know the thing is right.'

For Sir Lord Comic, the change in the style of 'toasting' in recent years is most strongly evident in the rhythm, especially the fact that you now have to follow the new rhythm in a much different way than before. 'In our days when the Ska was playing "Ska Ska...", we could go with the sound like "Chi Chi Chi..." Right? Now the sounds are 'doo doo do-do doo...' A guy says, "Ah born a natural D.J.", and he sings the rhythm. So these D.J.'s are just working to the rhythm and they find what they call lyric & lyrics & lyrics & more lyrics. So you have the D.J. lyrics fade, next D.J. steps forward... But these D.J.'s are very great.'

Of the new generation of D.J.'s/toasters, Count Machouki ranks U-Roy as 'the best of the crowd,' adding, 'I think he has got it the way I think it should really be done. That's the way I would like to find myself to do it – if I was still young – the way U-Roy did it,'

'But I still feel that I have contributed something to our Jamaican culture,' states Count Machouki, 'and I am proud. I cannot say that I have been financed for my efforts. But what I have accomplished, I know that a lot of my Jamaicans have been able to find a living by my idea. They make me feel pretty proud. I walk ten feet tall. Although I may not be as good as these guys today. People say I'm real great. But I'm humble.'

The Great 'U' Roy: *"Good timing is what it takes. And at the same time you have to have a voice that matches. To me, that's what this thing is all about."*

'"Now we'll give you the scene, you got to be real keen. And me no jelly bean. Sir Lord Comic answer his spinning wheel appeal, from his record machine. Stick around, be no clown. See what the boss is puttin' down." Those were the first words that I used.' – Sir Lord Comic.

Sir Lord Comic took Count Machouki's innovation a stage further, by toasting on the record. But before that, he started out as a regular dancer, a street dancer – or what in those days was called 'a legs man'. 'I used to follow a sound in Maxwell Avenue by the name of Admiral Deans. That was the same time as Duke Reid, Sir Coxsone, Tom (the Sebastian), Count Stitt... The D.J. at that time was Willy Penny; and I used to follow the sound and practised every day the new move. Because if you carry a move this Saturday, you cannot carry the same move next week. You have to have something new all the time. Now, the D.J. at that time was actually putting on records. He wasn't talking. Right?

'Well I was first inspired to become a D.J. by Count Machouki, who was the Number One D.J. at that time for Sir Coxsone's Downbeat. Machouki used to play the records and take up his mike and toast the people like "Love is real, Love is pure, Love is something that the doctor cannot cure", and everybody would say "Yeh!" So it occurred to me that the D.J. that could really talk should really have the edge over the other D.J.'s that just merely put out the records.

'So I started to track Willy Penny: see how he operates the amplifier, see what kind of selection he used to bring the crowd, see how he would cool down the crowd with certain tunes and things like that. I'd get to learn the name of the records. Sometimes when he felt like dancing, he'd say, "Comic, you can play that...", and I'd take the opportunity. Well it so happens that Christmas 1959, something happened fantastically. Willy Penny played at (-) off Maxwell Avenue. But he over-drank, so the boss, Mr Deans, says to me: "Comic, you think you can manage it?" I said I'd try. I was so enthused I went down to Spanish Town Road to borrow a mike from a man called Nat King Prof, a veteran of the Ska/Rock Steady/R & B scene. I told him that this is an opportunity I'd like to take in style. Well he lent me a Grampian mike.

'Well the 26th of December 1959, believe you me, it was from that time. I put on a record by Len Hope called, "Hop, Skip and Jump"; and when the tune started into about the fourth groove I says "BREAKS!" (Laughs) When I says "breaks" I have all eyes at the amplifier, y'know. And I says, "You love the life you live, and you live the life you love. This is Lord Comic," That night was exciting, very exciting. The music is playing and you are doing a thing like chicka-chup chicka-chup... Those types of things enthused the dancers.

'So we are very proud of ourselves to know that we had actually the opportunity to create it. I saw Machouki using a mike and I put it on a record. Right? In my own voice and became the first D.J. to record a song in Jamaica – "Adam and Eve went up my sleeve, and they didn't come down till Christmas Eve" – that was the title of it.'

'Good timing is what it takes. And at the same time you have to have a voice that matches. To me that's what this thing is all about.' – U-Roy.

Tommy McCook recalls first meeting the highly original (and now legendary) U-Roy back in the 1960s, at Duke Reid's Treasure Isle studio: 'Duke liked how he was doing the music live and decided to record him. Well U-Roy came to the studio with his lyrics and what he wanted to say, and he would sit down and make sound like "Wowww!". It was something for the whole of Jamaica. At one time he had three tunes in the chart at once, one-two-three – "Wear You to the Ball", "This Station Rule The Nation" and "Wake the Town and Tell the People". One-two-three on both radio stations. Nobody else could get in except at four. (Laughs) U-Roy had the three places booked for months. We liked it, we liked what was happening.'

McCook, who was in the band that backed U-Roy on these hits (the Supersonics), is now somewhat weary of the direction that D.Jing has since gone. 'The D.J.s are saying less these days and they are not talking things that one would like to hear all the time, y'know. But in those days, U-Roy was talking in between a singer. He knew he had so much time, so many seconds to say so many words, and he was saying a pile of words within those seconds – to cover back, to let the Paragons sing something, and back again. It was a different art form, much more exciting than now.'

U-Roy innovated the singing-talking form of toasting – wherein he talks in tune with the music, with the same pitch as the music, in a manner very similar to a singer. In addition, he transformed D.Jing into a medium of Rastafarian expression. In other words, he departed radically from the traditional fun-orientation of the earlier D.J.'s, who often used 'nonsense' statements for their effect, and instead focussed on political and cultural themes. His lyrics are laced with Biblical and religious references, chants to Africa, and 'curses' to Babylon. But he also uses humour. U-Roy is particularly careful in pointing out that his 'message' is universal, that D.Jing is a medium through which to speak to all people, not just black or white.

U-Roy carried the art form to newer heights, and by so doing opened the way for the contemporary generation of D.J.'s to emerge.

Right – Big Youth at rehearsals at Harry J's studios: *"Them have reggae music as a little dance music. But there's a form of reggae music called Jah music. Seen. That is music that inspire black people."* Facing – Big Youth in his Sensemelia field.

But at the same time he is not alienated from tradition. 'We used to have a lot of good D.J.'s before,' he says; 'we had King Stitt, Lord Comic, Count Machouki. Machouki was my favourite at the time.' And like Count Machouki, U-Roy seems to eschew the paraphernalia of stardom. Although at one time he became something of a cult figure and had numerous imitators – which prompted his celebrated caution: 'Do not imitate because I originate.'

U-Roy's originality reveals itself largely in his development of technique, his effective use of rhythmic phrasing which gives the lines a particularly sharp edge: 'Some D.J.'s don't want to deal with people. They only want to deal with Babylon alone. Or they want to deal with an individual set of people. But you must first realise this, if you're dealing international: If you can say "Fire BURN!", you might as well say, "For ALL Wicked!" and not just Some Wicked. Every wicked heart must feel this. You understand. It's not just "Fire Burn for One Wicked". Wicked near and afar must feel it. Yeah. Me don't want just "Fire Burn... England, or just England alone". "Fire BURN wicked ALL over Rome!" You understand. Yeah. It's true. It's the rhythm that I deal with in this thing.'

'Them have reggae music as a little dance music. But there's a form of reggae music called Jah music. Seen. That is the music that inspire black people. The music is philosophical, so much so that it brings people out of darkness. Jah music tells people about themselves.' – Big Youth

Count Machouki's earlier discovery that 'word is power', crystallises in the work of both U-Roy and Big Youth. In Jah music, that power lies in the message of Rastafari. 'Some people just deal with dream and fantasy,' says Big Youth, 'even within the same music them call reggae. Me listen to them, and me vexed with them 'cause they blow the youths' mind.' Big Youth's own discovery of this process led to him adopting an alternative vision, Rastafari, and using the toasting form as a direct means of extolling 'the culture of Jah'.

'Well me was a man used to love to go to dances;' he recounts, 'and we used to go to the dance and hear a whole lot of chants. More time I didn't love what they say. It was in 1968-9. That was when strongly I didn't like the kind of things that them say... How I see it, the man them talk too much about "Baby, Baby", while the people have a problem. It's a problem that everyone must face. And you have to show them and make them face up to the problem. You have to confront them, instead of telling them about the "Baby Baby" scene... because for me you have life, you have emotion, you can share a scene there. Then me thinks, Jah is our Creator. So let me tell the people some more about Jah. Through the same book, the Bible, is how we get to know we have our God, Jah.

'In desolation we really forget to come together for ourselves. Youths and youths. Because all dread things could happen to me too. So I just love to go out dancing and hold a mike and chant up to the Creator. Most men run from the truth, they don't want to hear too much about the Creator. They don't want to learn. They just want to live as the system teach them so.'

'Youth in the ghetto' is a recurrent theme in Big Youth's music. In fact, his primary concern is with youth, and his 'utterances' are aimed at counteracting the mental enslavement which he sees a lot of popular music (among other things) as having on youths' minds. There is a definite political edge here, although Big Youth himself would not put it quite in those terms. His use of certain political figures in the lyrics, for instance, has more a sense of 'the curse', than a specifically political intention: 'We have to do it. We have to use these figures because they are looked up. Call out their names!'

The underlying philosophy in Big Youth's music is 'the unification of mankind, the whole unification', a process which he believes is in reach. This universal perspective is also a logical extension of how Reggae music itself is understood: 'It is a peoples' music. I just deal with no one people. I deal with people throughout earth...who I deal with through inspiration and through humanity. Jah developed a music for me to reach out to people.'

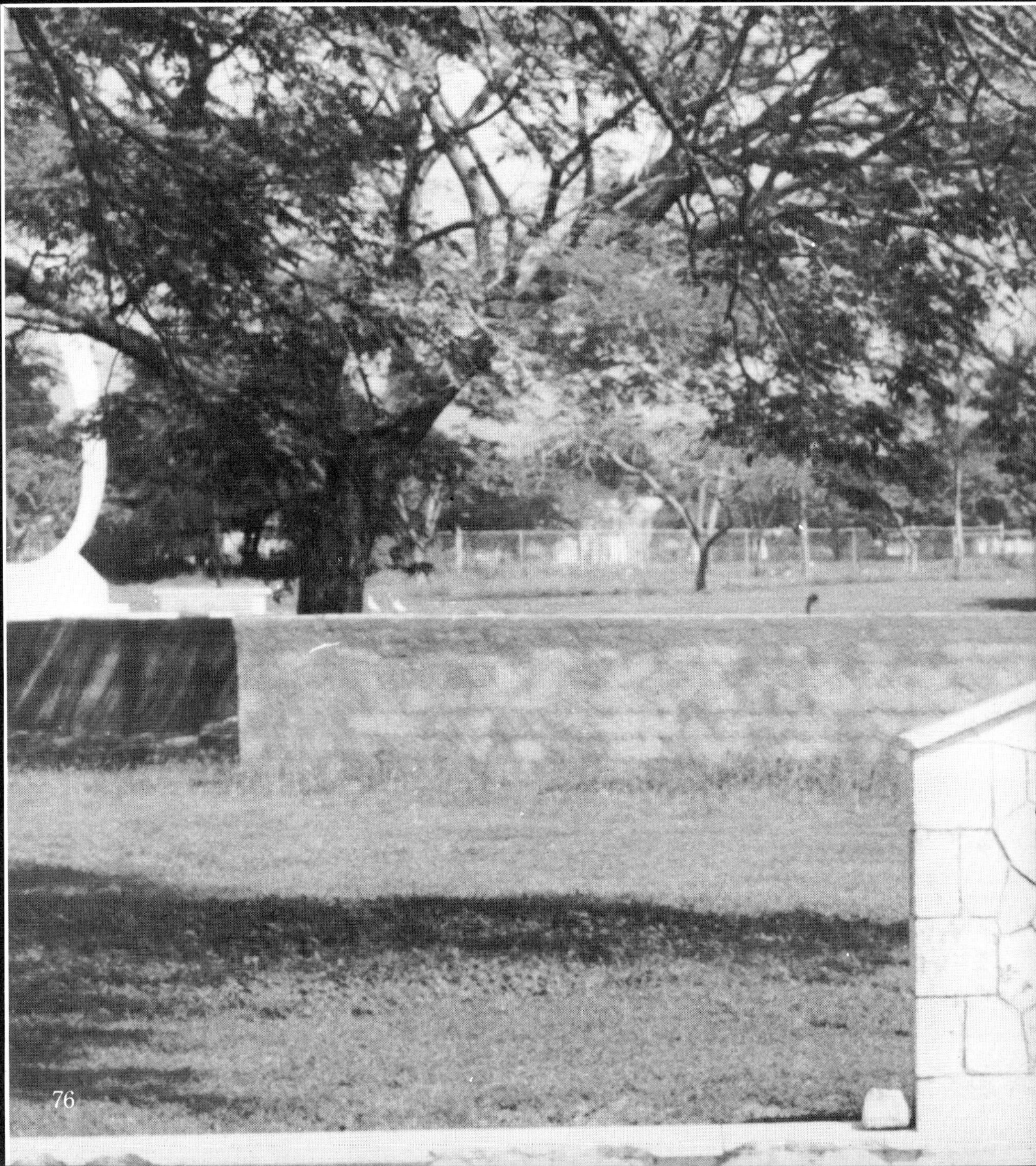

BLACK ARK, SPIRITUALITY & REGGAE

Right – **Marcus Garvey**. Facing – Emperor Haile Selassie the First, makes a point to the late Jamaican prime minister, Donald Sangster, on his triumphant visit to Jamaica in 1966.

'The Rastafarians have been the first people to express revolutionary ideas in music. And in this respect reggae music is also unique, in the Caribbean at least. Because you will find in Trinidadian calypso that you'll have songs of derision, you'll have songs of protest. But you don't have the singers expressing the revolutionary ideas that reggae singers express. And this has had the effect, I think, of politicising the population to a greater extent – because I don't think there is a more politicised population anywhere in the world than the Jamaican population.' – Pamela O'Gorman

The Rastafarian movement originated in Jamaica in the 1930s. It coincided with the crowning of Haile Selassie I as Emperor of Ethiopia, and it drew inspiration from the teachings of the Jamaican Black Nationalist leader, Marcus Mosiah Garvey. Rastafari represented a continuation of the old Afro-religious tradition which had been started by the Maroons, and it emerged as a form of religious expression charged with political significance. Rastafarian thought became the single most radical influence on the development of Jamaican political consciousness, particularly among the poorer sections of society, and at the same time it reinforced among followers of the faith a powerful sense of Black Spirituality. Its concepts and images have become the most vibrant elements in contemporary Jamaican political and cultural expression.

Marcus Garvey's Back-to-Africa Movement of the 1920s had stimulated black people's pride in their African heritage; it was a re-affirmation of black dignity and pride. Through his writings and speeches, Garvey set out to reconstruct both historical and Biblical knowledge from a specifically black point of view. For example, he reinstated the central part played by 'the Black race' in world history, by highlighting the fact that the ancient Egyptians and Ethiopians, who were originally a 'Black race', had great civilisations long before the Europeans. In accordance with his insistence on black pride, Garvey also reasserted the belief in a black God; although accepting in principle that God has no colour as such, Garvey was nonetheless acutely aware of the white God that the European-Christian tradition had created and imposed on the rest of the world.

Garvey urged black people to be self-reliant and self-sufficient; and to worship but one god – the God of Ethiopia – and to aim at one destiny – Africa. His international organisation, the Universal Negro Improvement Association (U.N.I.A.), which he set up in 1914, was probably the first black-created attempt in the Western world to carry out politically radical programmes for the benefit of black people. There is no doubt that Marcus Garvey succeeded in instilling into the minds of black people – not only in Jamaica, but in the United States and Africa as well – a new and dynamic sense of political and cultural awareness and direction. His impact was so great, in fact, that he was looked upon as a messiah, 'the prophet of

African redemption'. In 1916, when he left Jamaica for the United States, Garvey had prophesied: 'Look to Africa for the crowning of a Black King; he shall be the Redeemer.'

In 1930, the Prince Regent Ras Tafari was crowned Negus of Ethiopia. He took the name Haile Selassie ('Might of the Trinity'), to which was added the Biblical titles, 'King of Kings and Lord of Lords, Conquering Lion of the tribe of Judah, Elect of God and Light of the World'. This historical event was interpreted by the founders of the Rastafarian movement as the fulfilment of Marcus Garvey's prophecy.

The Rastafarians – whose name is a combination of 'Ras' (Head) and 'Tafari' (Prince) – began to examine the Bible more closely, fleshing out clues and directives which would eventually become the cornerstone of their theology. Although the Bible retained its significance as a holy book within the Rastafarian faith, the Rastafarians nevertheless believed that a careful re-reading of the scriptures was essential, because the Bible had been corrupted as the result of translation from its original Amharic language of Ethiopia. The Christian Bible, they further argued, only worked to undermine the integrity of black people, because it denied blacks their true god and their true place in history. At any rate, the Bible had been used as a weapon by the white masters against black people during slavery, and it continued to be used in this way up to the present. In other words, Christianity and the enslavement of the black race went hand-in-hand.

Thus the Rastafarians reinterpreted the Bible in Black terms; they reversed the meanings of the Biblical themes and symbols which had been projected by the dominant European-Christian tradition. 'Black' now symbolised purity and good, while 'White'

Top – Rasta preacher Pepe Judah at the Dunns River Falls. *"We've got to tell the people about Selassie-I."*
Bottom – Scully in the centre tells Pepe Judah about Rastafari and the days of the Skatalites.

represented evil. 'Sing unto God, sing praises unto His name: extol Him that rideth upon the heavens by His name JAH, and rejoice before Him' (Psalm 68:4). Hence the name 'Jah', the god of Rastafari, the omnipotent Black God who indwells in us all.

According to the Rastafarian faith, Haile Selassie is the living God and the Returned Messiah. The proof of this is revealed in the Book of Revelation, where the prophecy about the Emperor is made, and where the titles which Haile Selassie himself took on are also mentioned. The Rastafarians also believe that the Jesus referred to in the Bible is in fact Haile Selassie, and not the 'European' figure projected in Christian theology. The divinity of Haile Selassie is a centrally important element in the Rastafarian belief system, and for some people it is the most difficult one to handle. In any case, it has never been seriously undermined, even after the 'death' of the Emperor in 1975.

Rastafari maintains that the black person is the reincarnation of the ancient Israelites, who has been subjected to 'involuntary exile' by whites in Babylon (broadly, the oppressive capitalist/white world). Here, 'Israelites' is synonymous with 'Ethiopians' – i.e. they are Black. Babylon is Hell; whereas Ethiopia (or Africa) is both Heaven on earth and the 'ancestral' home of all Black people. Repatriation to Africa, which represents Black people's return to The Promised Land, is one of the principal demands often expressed in Rastafarian rhetoric. However, not all Rastas subscribe to repatriation, although they all do identify with Africa as the place where Black people belong, if not physically, at least 'spiritually'.

The Rastafarians also found a prophecy in the Book of Daniel which revealed that Black people will eventually rule the world. This is quite consistent with the general belief within Rastafarian theology of the essential superiority of the Black race. It has also helped to reinforce the near-total rejection among the more orthodox Brethren especially, of the dominant value-system of white Babylonian society. The sense of social and cultural exclusivity is very strong among the adherents of the Rastafarian faith. But it should be emphasised that Rastas themselves are generally not anti-white as such. They tend to adopt a highly philosophical stance and judge all people on the basis of their individual qualities. Rastas often say, 'I and I judge each man by his words and deeds.'

The most important meeting of the Rastafarians is called **Nyabingi** or **Grounation**. This is a large ceremonial occasion which brings together members of the cult from all over the island, like an association's national convention. It includes drumming, dancing, chanting and smoking the herb (ganja/marijuana). The Nyabingi dance of 'death and destruction' is thought to be to related to the Maroons dances of 'fire and power'. The Rastafarians' use of ganja has particularly attracted a lot of attention from the public, both in Jamaica and elsewhere, and it continues to be a primary target for attack by the authorities. Religious Rastas see smoking the herb ('the holy herb', as it is called in ritual contexts) as a purification of the body, where the body represents the 'church' in which the holy spirit indwells. This belief and practice contrasts sharply with the Catholic church, for example, where incense is used to purify the church building. Rastas cite passages from the Bible to prove that God sanctioned the use of the herb by mankind, and that smoking the herb is an integral part of the Rastafarian faith and way of life. The herb is held in high esteem even outside the esoteric confines of ritual.

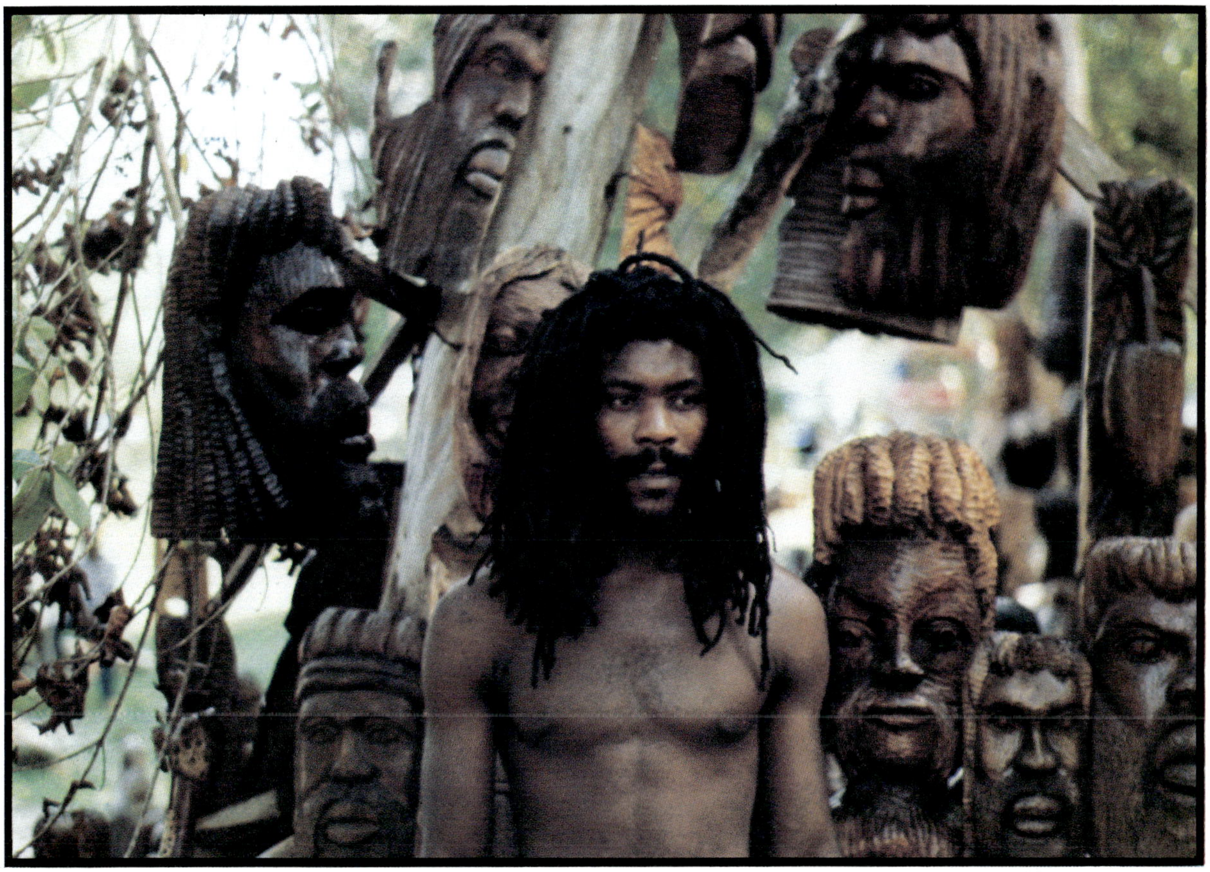

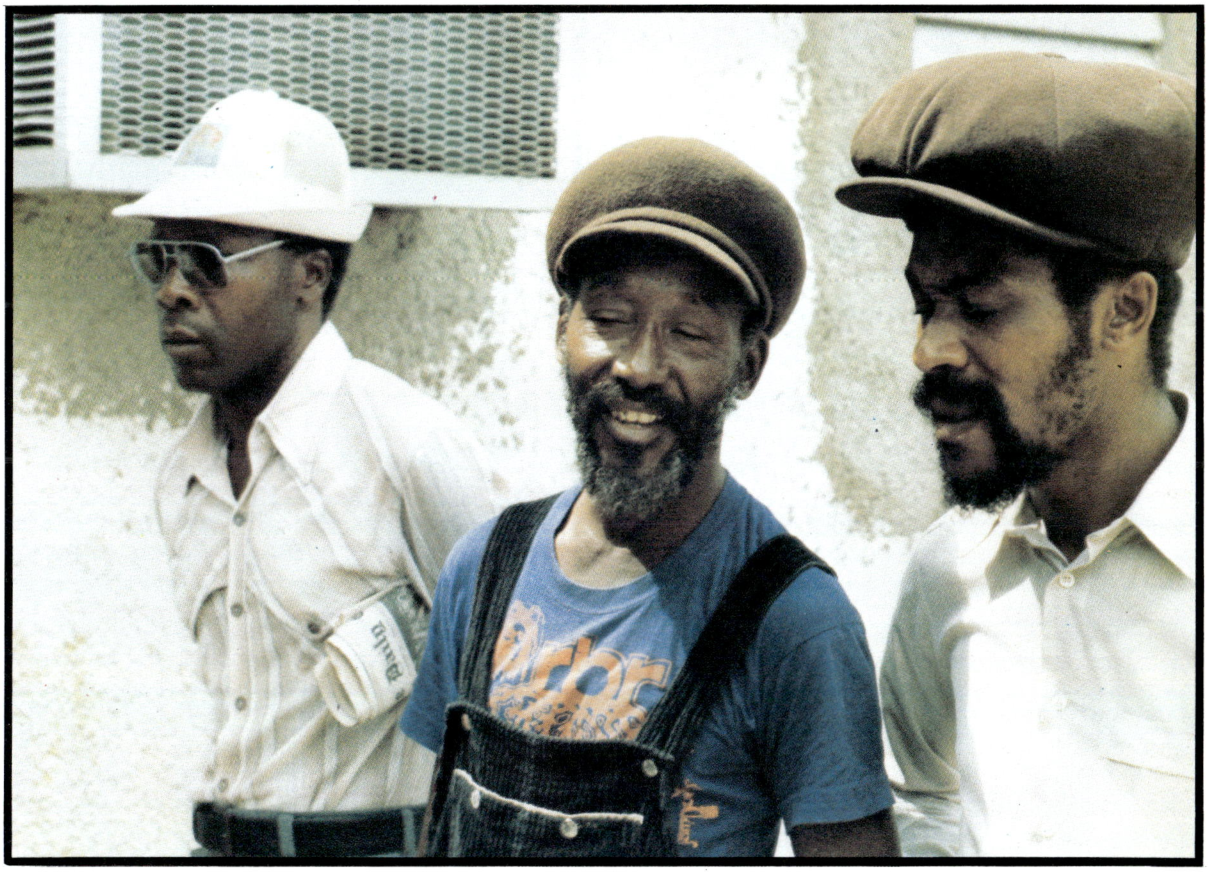

One of the most identifiable features of the Rastas is their long, naturally plaited hair-style or 'dreadlocks'. Wearing dreadlocks is considered by religious Rastas as 'wearing your crown', and it represents a defiance against the Babylonian system and a continuation of the African heritage. But the wearing of 'locks' does not necessarily mean that a person is a Rastafarian; nor do all Rastafarians necessarily wear locks. Dreadlocks are certainly an important sign of a person's black identity, and it may indicate a particular sympathy towards Rastafari or towards the radicalism which Rastafari represents. But Rastafarians themselves emphasise more the spirituality that underlies their beliefs and their way of life, and thus they tend to regard locks as merely part of a surface reality and not the essence itself.

In other parts of their lives as well, Rastafarians have adopted unique styles which not only sets them apart from the rest of the society, but also reinforces their own sense of strength and unity. The Rasta colours – Red, Green and Gold – which are the Ethopian national colours, appear on clothing, badges, walking sticks, musical instruments and so on. Rastas' dietary beliefs, to take another example, are closely related to the traditions of the ancient past: they discourage meat and avoid pork altogether. Rasta food is called 'I-tal food'; 'I-tal' is a Rasta word meaning 'things in their natural state'.

Rastafarian language is probably the most distinctive feature of the Rastafarian lifestyle. Rasta speech makes extensive use of metaphors and parables, Biblical and spiritual references, and terms and expressions which are derived from the ghetto roots experience. It is a highly expressive mode of communication; and though it uses English words, Rasta language reworks the standard meanings and usages of the words to create its own unique style. The best-known example of this is the expression 'I and I' which appears frequently in Rasta speech. It denotes 'oneself and the God that indwells within' – that is, it highlights the unity of the individual person and the omnipotent god, which is a fundamental principle in Rastafari. 'I and I' is used both in the singular and the plural sense; and in its plural usage (where, for example, it replaces 'you and me'), it encompasses the idea of the unity of all people.

In the 1940s, Rastafarian cultists left the urban areas to set up communes in the hill country. They patterned their newly-established isolated communities after the Maroons. The Rastafarian communes collapsed, however, following constant police raids and harassment by the authorities; although it re-started around the late 1940s and early 1950s. The authorities

Tommy McCook's drummers at a Nyabingi near Rock Fort.

continued to harass the Rastafarian community but this time the Rastas, who were now stigmatised by the establishment as 'outlaws', took stronger protective measures and withdrew deeper into the hill country.

It was around this time that a more extreme wing of the Rastafarian cult emerged – the Nyabingi Order or 'Locksmen', as they were called. It is thought that they were the first Rastas to wear the now familiar dreadlocks. The Rastafarians began to evolve more strongly African based forms of expression, especially in the area of music where they drew on the **Buru**, **Kumina** and Maroon traditions, as well as adopting elements from Afro-Christian Revival. The Rastafarians assumed the isolationist character of Maroon culture, and as such they became the vehicle through which the more African-oriented elements of Jamaican popular culture were maintained and developed. Strong elements of Rastafari were later absorbed into the contemporary urban context, which helped to shape the new 'roots' reggae of the 1960s to the present time.

'Over the years the Rastafarians have developed an individuality that in many respects is quite different from other cultural groups in Jamaica,' states Pamela O'Gorman. 'The Rastafarians, to a certain extent, have been in the forefront of Jamaican culture – simply because they of all people have cut themselves off from Western influences. They've looked inside themselves, and in being forced to look inside themselves, they have discovered something that nobody else has. So there is a pride and an individuality there that you are not going to find anywhere else in Jamaica. And the result has also been that they have introduced many innovations in art. You find in the visual arts particularly, that the Rastas have created an iconography of their own which is becoming well-known in Jamaica. Their speech of course has been very individual. And their music most of all. In the music, you're going to find that it is the drumming element that is alive and has been the most active.'

'The drum is the first sound that our foreparents used to send out messages with. Y'know all sounds, I feel, listen unto the drum, go with the drum, because that was the first sound before any electrical device. Our foreparents used to use that, y'know, send messages to one another, communicate with each other, just the drums, yeah **man!**' – Skully.

'Think what Count Ossie did using the same drums as the Buru people... He brought the music to a fine art. And he was a wonderful person.' – Olive Lewin

Right – **Lee Perry in boat.** Below – **Tommy McCook.** Bottom – **Brass section of The Skatalites at Harry J. Studio.**

Count Ossie, the legendary master drummer, was the founding father of modern Rastafari music. He frequently spoke of the importance of the drum in Jamaica's cultural history, and strongly influenced most of the drummers who were playing in the bands or as 'session' performers during his time. From as early as the late 1940s, he was holding jam-sessions at his mobile 'camp site' in the Wareika Hills area of Kingston, which attracted many of the outstanding jazz and popular musicians of the day – people like Don Drummond, Tommy McCook and Roland Alphonso. Count Ossie's early work with jazz musicians had inspired the formation of Count Ossie & the Mystic Revelation of Rastafari, an ensemble which combined jazz horn player Cedric Brooks and his Mystics band, with the Count Ossie Rastafarian Drummers. They were the most vibrant Rastafari band during the 1960s and 1970s, and made several Rastafari classics including the 'Grounations' album.

'Good evening and greetings. You people of the universe – this is Lee 'Scratch' Perry – Pipe Cock Jackson. Madder than the mad. Greater than the great. Rougher than the rough. Tougher than the tough. And badder than the baddest. We are here at the turntable terrnova; it means we are taking over. We're

taking over the air. We're taking over the mounts. We're taking over the star. We're taking over the sun. We're changing time. We're changing power. We're changing grace. We're changing space. We are doing things that His Majesty sent us to do in this Armageddon valley... in Jamaica.' – Lee 'Scratch' Perry

Lee 'Scratch' Perry is another seminal figure in the reggae 'roots' tradition. He started his career as a sound system operator and studio engineer for 'Coxsone' Dodd. He later moved on to set up his own Black Ark studio, and in 1968 he launched his 'Upsetter' label with the brilliantly produced classic 'People Funny Boy', a tune loaded with personal significance. He is also known as 'Pipe Cock Jackson' and 'The Mighty Upsetter'. His recording techniques, his experiments with sound effects and unusual rhythms, and his use of hard-hitting lyrics and singing, became trademarks of his productions. Many of his 'Upsetter' records in the late 1960s and early 1970s became chart-breakers.

At his Black Ark recording studio, Lee 'Scratch' Perry teamed up with people like the late Bob Marley to produce some of the most interesting and revolutionary work with the Wailers. He produced albums like 'Soul Rebel', 'African Herbsman', 'Rastaman Revolution'; and he gave the name to Marley's record company, Tuff Gong. Lee Perry produced a long line of famous songs including 'Small Axe', 'Funky Reggae Party', 'Duppy Conquerer', 'Fussin & Fightin', '400 Years' and others. Lee 'Scratch' Perry is one of the few surviving geniuses in the recording industry today. And he was Bob Marley's greatest mentor.

Lee 'Scratch' Perry's long exhortation (below) invokes both the apocalyptic and the uplifting themes, images and rhythms of

Lee Perry reaches for Excaliber the Sword of Fire.

Rastafari – laced with unexpected references to himself and music. He is the original Buru-man, Myalk-man, Obeah-man, mystical comedian and philosopher – all rolled up into one:

'Greetings in the name of the Father, greetings in the name of the Son, greetings in the name of the Holy Spirit. Hear the revelation of Ras Tafari, Emperor Haile Selassie-I, the King of Kings, the Lord of Lords. I'm standing in this spot where they used to transport slavery from Africa, to sail to Jamaica where the white plantation is. But it will be no more, as lightning liveth and thunderball rolleth. He that rideth the white horse in Revelation 22 say: "Time for the Black man to take over; time for the Black man to drive big car; time for the Black man to own big ship; time for the Black man to own aeroplane; time for the white man to work for the Black man." A change in time, says the miracle to Jesus.

'Version Two. May I introduce myself; my name is David, the heart of stone. My father is Samson who slew the Philistines with a donkey jawbone; and I am he who must slay Goliath with a sling and a stone, here at the seventh seal – in my hand, my microphone.

'We still talking about slavery. These are my proof that slavery up. I've got the seventh seal in my hand, formed by stone, the stone that King David used to, y'know, slew big Goliath. And the ruling power is this little stone, it's carved a K on it, that mean I am the f... King. Who loveth live, and who hateth gonna surely die. Well I am here to free all the people from mental slavery. I am to fulfil the book where Bob Marley left off. I *was* the teacher, and I am still the teacher.

'Talking about Black man redemption. Talking about freedom for the Black people. Talking about love and respect. Talking about truth. Talking about love. Talking about down with the hypocrisy. Talking about down with the government of wrongs. The government of wrong. Talking about up with truth; up with righteousness; up with L O V E. That's it.

'Talking about King Arthur, the best super-balancer, the best super-mixer, the best teacher, the best architect, the world international supreme. Black Art. The power lies in the bass. Toom, toom. Boom, boom. Talking about music Excalibur that was given to King David to

Lee Perry tells young girl of love and things, as Niney the observer looks on.

slaughter all his enemy. Excalibur, the sword of fire. We, the black people, must rule the universe – it is a compulsory. Yeah, I'm talking about Kalimus is a must. And when you work with me you got to be fast, I don't deal with amateurs.

'Sounds. Power. Magic. We call it Black Magic that control the world. Some call it reggae explosion. But I call it Deep Roots Music – the crown of the King, Emperor Haile Selassie. So I'm telling you about the power of the Black man. Sounds, words and power conquer all. As seventy-two nations must bow to reggae music, rock steady music, ska music, meringue music, calypso music, jazz music – don't care what the music might be, but music is the only comforter, I'm telling you the truth, man.'

'Me discover Rastafari from a long time but me never know its name. Me knew me's a Rastafari. Me used to love to read the Bible from a long time, before any religious thing. Me used to love it as a history book and as culture. I check it out and sight it out and read. And it states all things like Moses was a Black man, David was a Black man, Jesus was a Black man. Seen. And then the Book start showing me how old the throne of Africa is, and I started reading other books as compared to the Bible. And I found that Black civilisation was stronger from a longer period than white civilisation..

'Them never teach us that at school. Matter of fact, until this day most of the history they teach about Jamaica is about Christopher Columbus and Buccaneer and Pirate... Me never hear about Black man in a school. Tarzan swing on tree and beat up Black man and things like that, that's all they teach us about I and I. And none of it is true. Rastafari

Above – **Judy Mowatt** of the I-Threes. Right – **Bob Marley** caught in the act at Brighton Pavilion, 1980. Below – **The I Threes** caught in the act at Brighton Pavilion, 1980. Facing, Bottom – **Bob Marley** backstage at Crystal Palace, the last British concert.

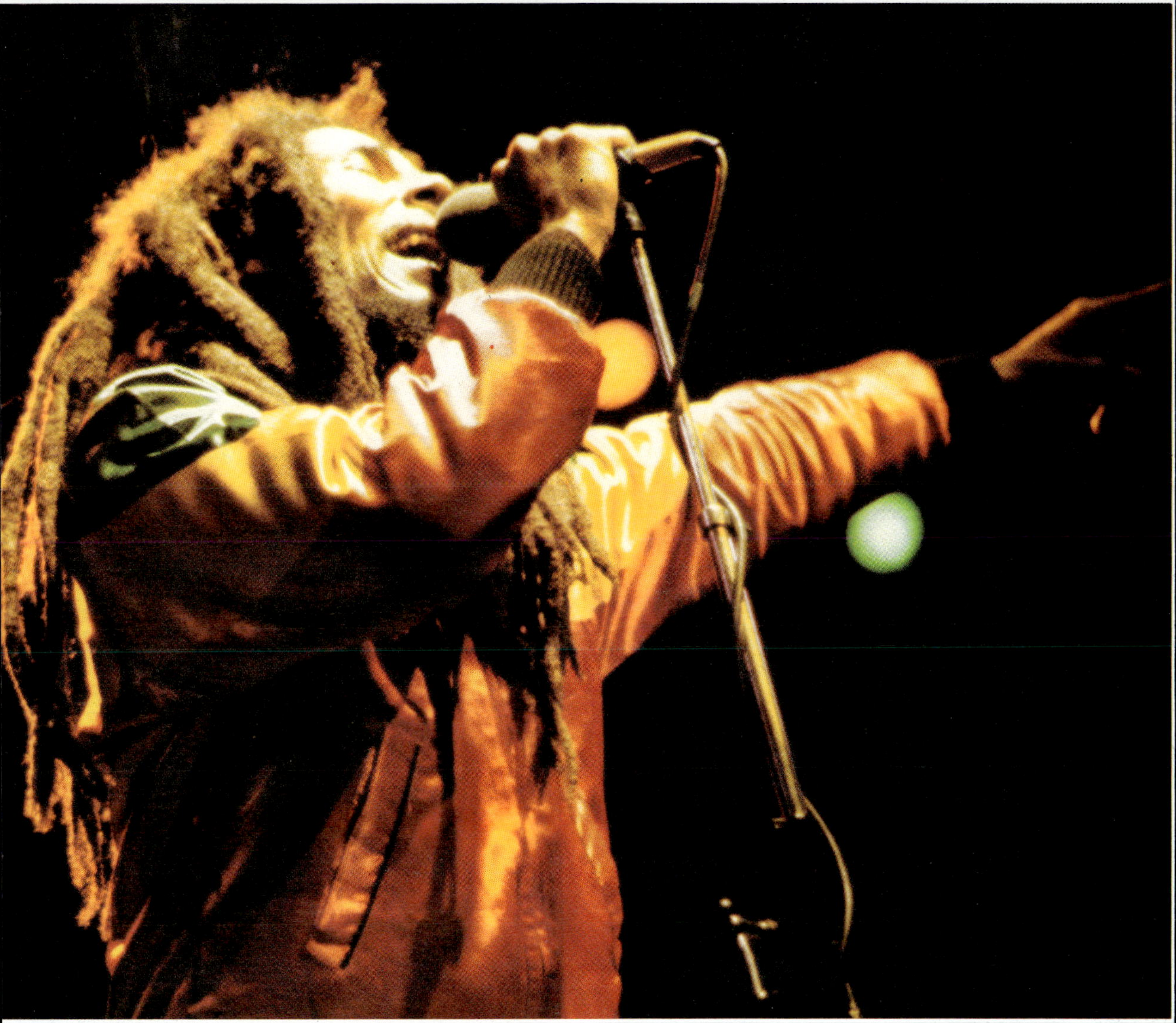

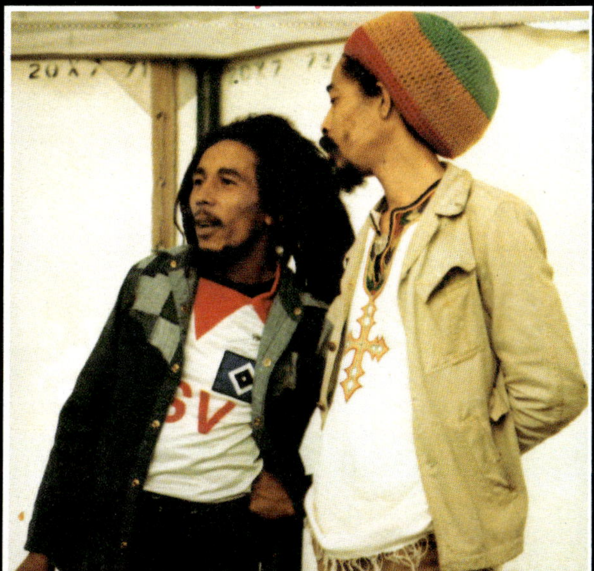

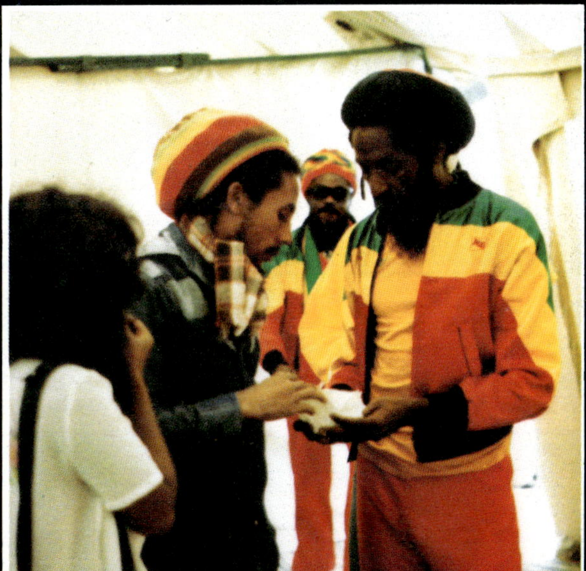

helped I to find I-self and I and I great Black heritage. Seen.' – Jimmy Riley.

Jimmy Riley, the outstanding political lyricist and singer, came on the music scene in the late 1960s. He made his first record for Duke Reid as a backing singer in The Sensations, a group that did mainly stage shows. He then joined The Uniques, which was led by the late Slim Smith, the greatest ballad singer of the Rock Steady/ early Reggae period. Jimmy Riley acknowledges that his own style was greatly influenced by Slim Smith; and their classic hit 'Sweet Conversation' exemplified the relaxed blending of musical approaches which typified the period: R & B style of vocalisation with a Jamaican Rock Steady rhythm guitar backing.

After a period with Bunny Lee, Jimmy Riley decided to go independent and to break away from the bind where the artist always has to go to the producer for money. He became a producer in the early 1970s, producing mostly singles. He also continued to write hit songs for other singers, such as 'Blinded By Love' (Slim Smith) and 'Can't Complain' (Delroy Wilson). His 'Tell the Youths the Truth' was a sharp indictment of the Babylonian education system that 'miseducates' black youths and deprives them of discovering their African heritage; while his 'Poor Immigrants' highlighted the plight of black people coming to Europe and America to work in badly paid, slavery-like jobs.

Jimmy Riley recalls a particularly memorable experience in his life, and indeed for every Rastafarian at the time – the visit to Jamaica of Emperor Haile Selassie in January 1966. Exuberant Rastas came from all over the island to welcome the Emperor. They crowded excitedly onto the tarmac as the Emperor descended from his plane, they lined the streets,

Lee Perry in Heroes' Park

and they rejoiced in the presence of the King.

'I was there. As a matter of fact, I saw Selassie at the University of the West Indies giving a speech one evening. I saw Selassie and I'm telling you, until this day I have never experienced anything like that or seen anything like that. The closest thing I'd say compared to Selassie him coming was the funeral of Bob Marley – where so many people pour out for a great occasion. And you know what I mean, the whole thing was like a great vibration of I and I coming together. That greatest there – although you can't compare life to death. But I mean the turn-out and the enthusiasm of the people was the closest thing to a miracle. Selassie's visit was a different and a greater thing because it was a happy occasion. Many people coming together to see I and I King. There's never been anything like that in Jamaica since.'

The evils of Babylon is a recurring motif in Rasta thought and music. The lyrics invoke Biblical themes such as 'retribution for the Wicked' and 'Fire', God's own final solution, which has become a powerful concept in Rastafarian vocabulary. For the Rasta lyricist, there is the pressing desire to leave Babylon: Babylon is no place for the Black person; Babylon is the force of oppression; Babylon is oppressive to I and I – Stepping out of Babylon is I and I desire. Seen. These are the constant themes and images expressed in Rasta lyrics.

'Africa? Africa? Africa? Just the mention of it, man, is like you call my name. Africa is the motherland and Africa is where we rightfully belong – and that's where I want to be.' – Dennis Brown

Dennis Brown, one of the top Rasta-reggae artists in Jamaica today, started singing and making records professionally when he was 13 years old. He started with Coxsone Dodd's Downbeat, where he met many of the giants of the day. It was an exhilarating experience for any talented young artist setting out on a career in music:

'Working with Downbeat was like going to a college because you had all the people that was happening at that time there. They had people like Alton Ellis, The Heptones, Lascelles Perkins, Lloyd James and John Holt. Coxsone was the ace producer at the time, y'now, and that was where everything was happening. So if you were coming through Downbeat's school things would really happen there. My first song with Downbeat was "No Man is an Island".

'Well at the time you had people like Lou Rawls. Lou Rawls had a lot of influence on me. And you had people like Nat 'King' Cole and groups like The Temptations and a group called The Delphonics. Well, somehow I think my style is a very unique one, wherein I always try to improvise. I don't just try and sing one way all the time, I improvise as much as possible. And with that you find I created a very unique style.'

'Well Rastafarian philosophy is my life – that is like my whole life from the beginning, y'know, the way I grew up and the way I live – my lifestyle is just Rasta. It wasn't until I visited England wherein I got the chance of learning how to differentiate what was really religion. In England you see that the Jews have got their own religion and they stick to their culture, the Greeks the same, the Pakistani, the French, the Dutch – you know, they all live their culture. Well I saw wherein it was possible and would be wise for me to identify myself with being a Rasta. You can still be a Rasta and not have your dreadlocks, y'know. But I had to identify myself,

91

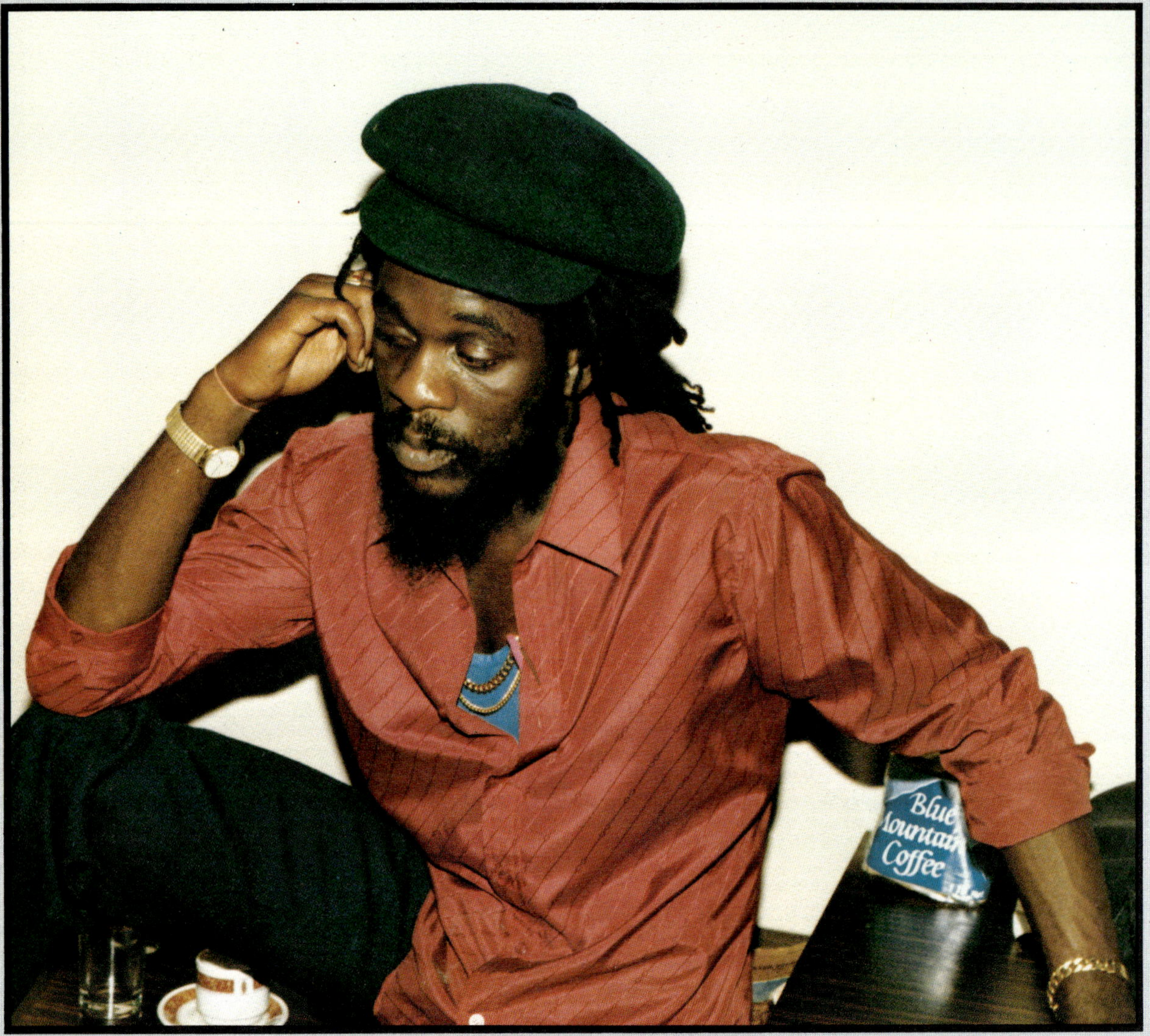
Blue
Coffee

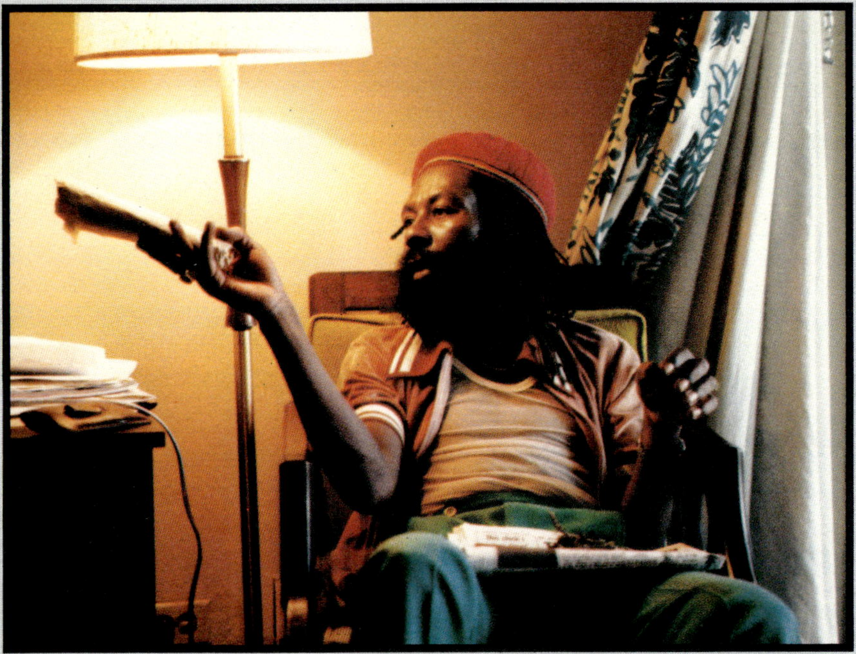

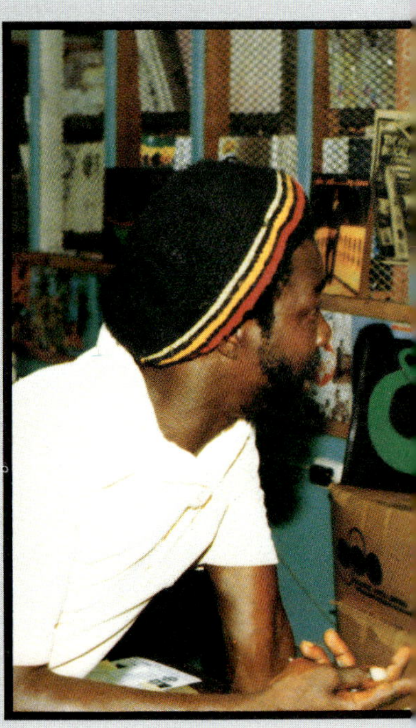

Clockwise from above – **Miss Lou** sits in her backyard talking about folk music and Dinkey Minnie. The beautiful **Sheila Hylton** performing at Harry J's Studio. **Jah Jerry** outside Harry J's Studio drinking a Red Strip beer. **Charlie Ace** buying records from Neville Lee, at Sonic Sounds. The Great **U. Roy** rolls a spliff off Sensimilla. **Dennis Brown**, black prince of reggae.

93

that means to make it be known – say, yes, D. Brown is a Rasta.'

Love is a prominent theme in many of Dennis Brown's songs, and it is a topic which many people identify with. This was reflected in the success of 'Money In My Pocket', which not only was a big hit in England, but also got Dennis Brown invited to the 1979 Montreux Jazz Festival. It was the first time that a jazz festival had a reggae slot, and it included Peter Tosh and Steel Pulse. Dennis Brown remembers it as 'a historical event, one of the greatest events I can remember.

'Well, yeah man, when I sing about love I find within myself that there comes a time when you have to move away from that and sing about awareness, consciousness, liberated music like Black Liberation. I love Black people... not that I am prejudiced, you know. But what I fight against is all the racialism and prejudice, pride and arrogancy and evil ways.'

Dennis Brown sees the singer as a kind of preacher, who expresses a message to the people through song and lyrics. His 'Wolf and Leopard', which was inspired by Biblical imagery, is a very good example of a Rasta 'morality' song which has global implications.

'The lyrics for "Wolf and Leopard" came about through vibes, y'know, when we were in the studio. The rhythm wasn't originally made for "Wolf and Leopard". At the same time we were in the studio laying down the rhythm, which was on a two-track, we were around by Lee Perry's studio, Black Ark Studio, and they were playing it and we were saying "yes, this rhythm *nice*". So we made up the song.

'...You see, we are living in an environment now that you find a lot of wolves, a lot of informers, tale-bearers, y'know, murderers, sorcerers, thieves, liars – and believe me, I

Big Youth, Dennis Brown and Delroy Wilson share a joke outside Joe Gibb's studio.

never thought that in this time you'd really find liars, but up to the other day, yesterday, too true. Up to the other day I find a man tell I a lie and swear upon Jah's name, y'know sir, swear upon Jah's name, about how much Jah can paralyse him if him so and so on... When I check it out, the man was lying!'

Righteous indignation forms an important part of the broader attack on Babylon, it attacks the sort of attitudes and behaviours which Babylonian culture instills into people. For the Rasta musician – and many conscious reggae artists generally – music is capable of penetrating the forces of evil. Music purifies the soul. Black Spirituality looms large in all this, because it is the guiding principle in Black musical creativity. Marcia Griffiths, former singer with the I-Threes, the female trio that used to back Bob Marley, is in no doubt about the 'spiritual force' that lies behind reggae music. 'Because our music is truth and it is positive,' she says, 'so it definitely has a spiritual force and the message is there.'

Marcia Griffiths acknowledges the importance of Africa in the history of reggae music but, like other Jamaican artists rooted in the religious/spiritual tradition, she also believes that the music has to reach far beyond even Africa:

'Music is music and you can't put a label to it, because it is music and we are all players and singers for the Almighty God. And I think we should spread this all over the world, Africa and everywhere else, and give thanks to Bob Marley that we were part of it and were able to go all over the world to spread the music and try to let people know that apart from just saying reggae music, it is a music that gives feeling and reaches the soul. Any music can do that and any singer, if it's coming with truth.'

'This music, reggae music,' says Skully, veteran musician from the Ska days and rootsman, 'tell we A tell the world, y'know – telepathically and physically and mentally and spiritually – that we tell the truth. This music here what I and I create down the Western Hemisphere here, has to cover the whole four corners of the world and tell every man, woman and pickney that they must know themselves, and know who is God.'

Rastafari has sharpened the political edge to large areas of contemporary reggae music; and it has also nourished, with perhaps even greater intensity, the religious and spiritual roots of the music. Harry J. sums it up simply when he says, 'Reggae is a gift from Jah to the Jamaican people.' The deep roots of reggae are embedded in this statement.

Gregory Issacs inside his Africa Museum Record Shop.

MONEY IN MY POCKET

Harry J standing outside his studio: *"Reggae music is going in the right direction and it's going to take its rightful place in the world of popular music."*

'Reggae music is going in the right direction, and it's going to take its rightful place in the world of popular music. One of the reasons why it hasn't got bigger – our problem is marketing, not from the Jamaican point of view, but from the major companies abroad who refuse to market the records because they spend millions of dollars developing their own music. They only try to market reggae music that they have under their control; they try to create a concept with this music, and try to pitch an image of Jamaicans which I personally don't like. Because it is not the true image of the Jamaicans.' – Harry J

The Jamaican record industry grew out of the activities of the early sound systems. During the late 1940s and early 1950s, sound system operators had built up a large following especially among the poorer sections (i.e. the majority) of the Jamaican population. This laid the foundation for later developments in popular music. Initially, the sounds relied heavily on imported R & B records. This kind of music was very successful in Jamaica at the time. But when in the late 1950s the bottom of the R & B market fell out and the records became less available, the Jamaican sound system men quickly filled the gap and started producing their own records for local consumption. This coincided with the arrival of Ska, the first wholly indigenous popular music produced by Jamaicans.

The music scene gained momentum by the early 1960s. The producers started to build their own recording studios, record manufacturers and other ancillary operations were set up, and so on. 'So you have promoters; you have an audience willing to participate in the form of going to the dances and buying records; you have a growing flock of singers and musicians ready to perform, and skilled enough to be recorded and to make up the travelling bands which would play at nightclubs and dances throughout the urban areas and some parts of the rural area. All this,' concludes Garth White, 'leads to the development of a fairly thriving recording industry in Jamaica.'

Of course the business was still controlled by a handful of energetic promoters, and there was the same rivalry that existed in the early sound system days. But the difference was the amount of capital that was tied up in the business, which required more sophisticated practices than before, and the fact that there was a pool of local musical talent which the promoters/producers vied for. Not surprisingly, the artists themselves were often drawn into what guitarist Bobby Aitkens described as 'the rat race business... the cut-throat thing, with everybody pushing and pushing, and the bigger fish having the bigger bite.'

There are numerous accounts of rip-offs, shady deals, strong-arm tactics and blatant exploitation; but these are hardly unique to the Jamaican experience. In fact, the social and professional network is such in the island that few people allow themselves to be absorbed by the uglier side of events and prefer simply to carry on with their own creativity, perhaps taking the occasional swipe in lyrics.

The advent of the popular music industry in Jamaica coincided with the Ska/Rock Steady explosion of the late fifties and early sixties. And these two events were propelled by the new thrust of national identity which had culminated with Jamaican independence in 1962. The new government lent its support, not only by discouraging the importation of foreign music, but also by taking measures to protect the viability of the indigenous music industry. For example, Edward Seaga recalls how early efforts

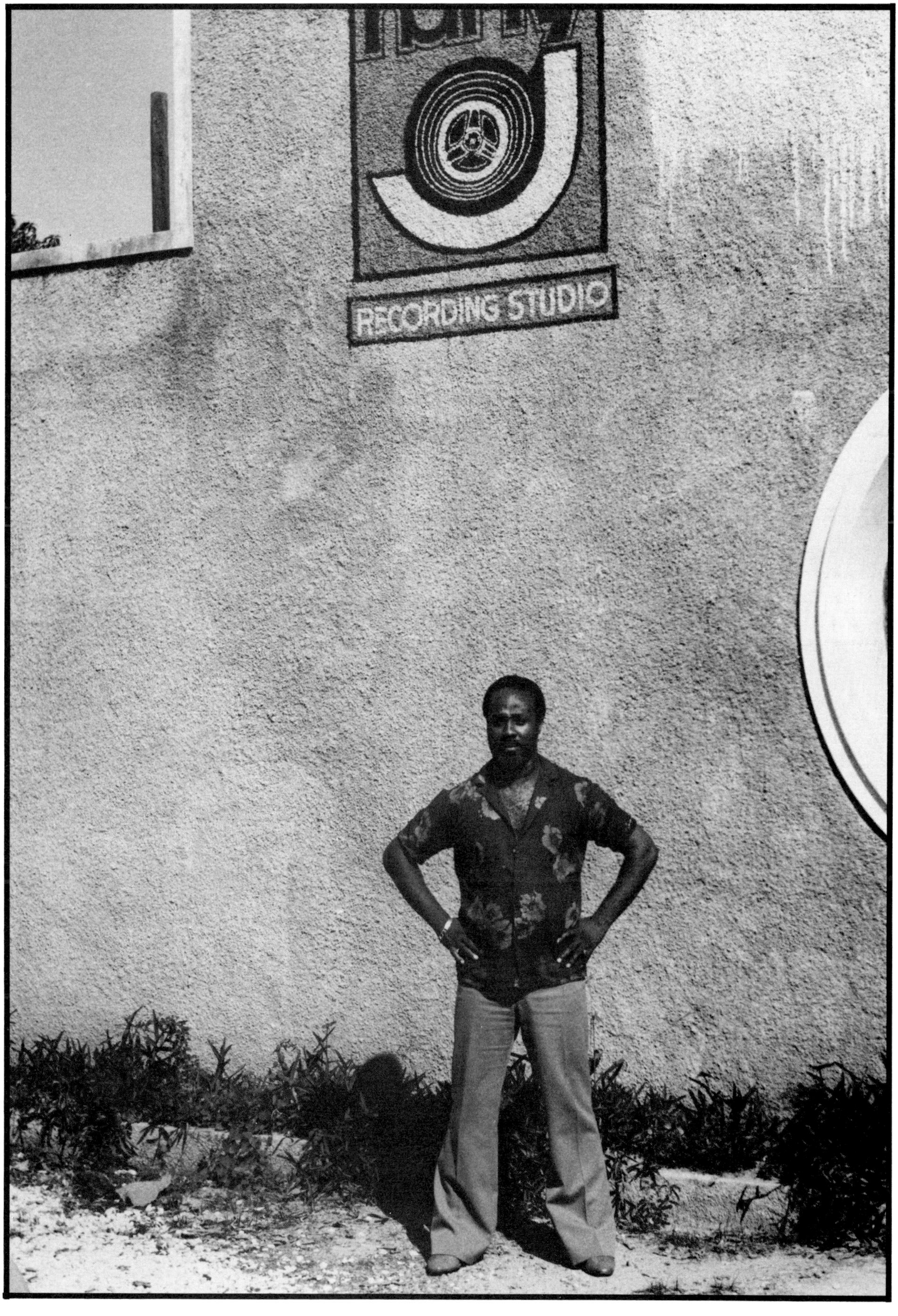
RECORDING STUDIO

were made to protect the artists' performing rights:

'What we developed for Jamaican musicians was not only the opportunity to produce songs for the local market, but to expose these songs for an external market. In the early 1960s, when the Ska came on the scene, we recognised that there was going to be a need to protect performing rights. We were able to do so by getting a government agency appointed here as a representative of the Performing Right Society [a British-based agency which grants performing licences and collects royalties on behalf of its members]. This gave us the opportunity to have a bigger share of the pool of funds that go to the P.R.S., which could then be shared among the local artists. These are the steps we have taken, and we're going to take many more,' continues Mr Seaga, 'because in our Cultural Development Commission we have appointed people who have this background and who have the capabilities of taking further steps to protect the artist, the writer and the performer.'

Copyright ownership was another area that became crucially important, as Edward Seaga again explains: 'We found that in the market practices here, that there were a number of problems arising out of copyright ownership. And in particular, when folk songs were used as the base, when sufficient changes were made so that they were no longer in the public domain but could be copyrighted as the work of an individual writer, we found that there were many claims and counter-claims, and so on.'

Jamaican popular music started to reach a wider audience by the mid-1960s. Britain was one of the main outlets, with people like Chris Blackwell (Island Records) and Lee Goptal (Trojan Records) importing records on a large scale and producing artists as well. In Jamaica itself, the recording business was still linked to the servicing of sound systems, which a number of producers still operated. But there was now a definite impulse towards developing external markets for their music.

The arrival of Reggae in the late 1960s established 'the Jamaican sound' firmly on the international popular music scene. But it also opened up a new set of problems for both the artists and the producers, particularly in the area of commercialisation. The Jamaican music people are committed, on the one hand, to maintaining and promoting the essential and unique qualities of Jamaican music; while on the other hand, they are having to come to terms with the demands and/or prejudices of the wider commercial arena.

Singers stand outside African Museum Record Shop in Idlers Rest.

Harry J's comment quoted at the beginning of the chapter, pinpoints the nature of the problem faced by the Jamaican music industry today.

One dimension of the problem stems from the way that white companies tend to promote reggae music abroad; especially the false impressions they create of the music and of Jamaicans generally, for instance, in album covers showing palm trees and sunshine etc. This image is sold to foreign audiences, many of whom accept it as reality. 'Now the problem,' says Harry J., 'is when the foreigners and tourists come here and discover that Jamaicans do not actually live like the impressions created by the white companies and media. All this idea of it being drug music or criminal music... right? This is one of our big problems in the reggae business, overcoming these false impressions about the music and the people.'

A great deal of pressure is put on reggae artists as well. For example, singers or musicians who make a big hit in Jamaica may well find themselves lured away by the big companies with the promise of more lucrative pickings on the American or European scene. And as if money isn't a sufficient enough bait, there is the additional pitch that 'the Jamaican sound' can be better reproduced in technically superior American and European studios! There are also numerous instances where a reggae record is produced in Jamaica, then taken abroad where it is 'doctored' or re-mixed, and released in a rather bland form that is apparently more suitable for white audiences. Many Jamaican producers and artists complain about these exploitative practices, which they believe can be effectively countered by the authentic music which continues to come out of Jamaica.

'The whole thing lies within the market,' states Harry J, who is one of the most successful of the new generation of Jamaican producers on the scene today, 'And people are going to have to watch the market in which their records are being marketed.' This emphasis on marketing grew out of Harry J's early experiences as an independent producer and especially his background as an insurance salesman. He had realised very early in his career that the main problem for the producer was actually getting records into the shops and sold. He adopted an approach which was ingenious, to say the least.

Harry J started his career in the music business by forming a band in 1963. Not long after, the other musicians decided to leave, to go off and study. 'And I was left with the responsibility of paying off all the instruments,' recalls Harry J, 'and I had to work hard. I started to work as an insurance salesman, and I built up a credit reference. I swore at the time that I would never get involved in music unless I have enough money.' He eventually saved enough money to enable him to promote a record on his own, and so he became an independent producer. He produced his first record in 1968 at Coxsone's studio, 'No More Heartaches', which became one of the first Reggae hits.

'How the "reggae" came about,' says Harry J, 'is that we did this rhythm song and I thought the organ was light in it. So I decided to rent a special organ, a Hammond organ. We used a two-track recording – all the instruments and voice were put on one track, and a reggae riff with an organ on the other track. The record was unusual and it became one of the big hits... and it started the reggae movement in England.'

Harry J's initial success in the recording business was largely due to his keen sense of salesmanship, which no doubt had been developed during his insurance days. This was put to the test when 'No More Heartaches' first came out. 'I had problems because nobody knew me in the recording business. I can remember an experience one day going into a record shop and asking them to buy a copy of the record, and them refusing. (This was the time when record shops used to take records on consignment.) I remember having on my jacket and tie and dancing in the sun. This lady came up and asked me for a copy and I says, "Well unless the shop could take six of them." Well the lady must have felt sorry for me or thought I was crazy dancing in the hot sun like this.'

Another effective ploy which Harry J adopted was to stop his car in front of the generally crowded Half Way Tree bus stop, as if it had broken down, and turn the radio up full blast when his record was playing. After a while 'People hearing it started to think that this particular record is being loved by the radio station. Because of my selling ability I felt that I had to start thinking big, thinking of the music going out to be an international music. I think I was responsible for the first movement in that direction.'

Harry J came to England to promote his next big hit, 'The Liquidator', which he had produced with Lee 'Scratch' Perry in 1969. Again his approach was ingenious: he managed to get the record played on B.B.C. radio's popular Tony Blackburn morning show. Then came another hit, the timely 'Young, Gifted and Black', sung by Bob (Andy) and Marcia (Griffiths). This was the first reggae record to use strings.

In 1971, Harry J set up his own recording studio, which a friend had designed for him. Though not sporting super-sophisticated equipment, it is considered one of the best 'sounding' studios in Jamaica today. Bob Marley recorded several albums there, including 'Catch a Fire' and 'Burning'. Harry J later formed a close association with Chris Blackwell (Island Records) and was instrumental in persuading Blackwell to promote Marley on an international scale. He was equally concerned about the way that reggae music generally was being promoted in England at the time:

'I could see that Chris was dedicated to the music, to promote reggae music. And I'd sit with him and explain the problem that whenever he personally is there, the people work; but when he left all they were interested in is pop, rock music in England... I'd explain to them (Island Records) that they should treat the music better, and that I think the music is as good as any other music, and that we (the Jamaican producers) notice that whenever Chris is not around nobody concentrates on reggae.'

Promoting reggae on the international scene obviously involves a certain amount of commercialisation. Producers and artists who are committed to this broader marketing strategy are very aware of the dangers, but they

Johnny Clarke, Pepe Judah and Prince Jazzbo in Bunny Lee's back yard.

nevertheless believe that a balance can be struck – between what is commercially viable (and necessary?) and what is authentic or coming from the roots. 'It is a genuine music,' argues Harry J, 'and it will continue to be so. Anybody who feels it is not continuing in that direction – it is just the feeling, you might be getting old. But the music, I don't think the music has changed. It might use more sophisticated recording techniques, etc., but the same basic feel remains, and it is only created here in Jamaica by the Jamaican people. I don't care where you go, you just don't feel reggae music like when you're creating it in Jamaica. This music is a gift to the Jamaican people.'

The Jamaican audience remains a key factor in the development of reggae music. However much the music goes out into the big wide world, the final judges of its authenticity and relevance are the Jamaican people themselves. This is something that many reggae promotors and artists express, and it is seen as being an essential part of their own creativity. Very often they will invoke a kind of cultural spirituality, which is seen to be rooted in the Jamaican ghetto and/or country experience. It is a constant reference point against which the music (and other art expressions) is assessed and defined. Harry J. sums it up with the old adage that 'you can take the man from the country, but you can't take the country out of him.'

Money is still a powerful force that has to reckoned with. And as Harry J, among others, constantly points out, the Jamaican market alone is nowhere near as substantial as (say) the American, where an artist can expect to reach a very large number of people and therefore be more or less viable commercially. There is no doubt, though, that Bob Marley's phenomenal success generated a lot of interest in reggae music throughout the world, and that it helped to fuel the growth of the indigenous Jamaican music industry. But at the same time it has also led to more artists, rightly or wrongly, expecting higher fees for their services. Many of them have even started producing their own records, although this fairly recent development hasn't really undermined the well-established position of the producer/promoter in the business. Nevertheless, the recording business has become increasingly more expensive to operate, despite, (or, maybe, because of) its growing popularity.

'I came into this business because of the satisfaction I get from doing certain things. I didn't come for the money,' says Harry J, who seems to be one of the few producers who has managed to keep a good name in the business. 'I didn't believe in greediness or in ripping off artists. Everytime I've recorded an artist, I've made him or her independent. They share in the profits. I did it with Bob & Marcia, I did it with the Heptones... And I can be proud that Lorna Bennett became a lawyer because of what I've done with the one record she did for me, 'Breakfast in Bed', which enabled her to pay her way through university.'

'The music has certainly progressed from being a local sound to an international sound. I've just come back from the EMI Conference in London, where we had forty-four delegates from about thirty countries. And one of the most interesting points that came up was that Jamaica was the only country, apart from Britain and America, who could say we have an international sound. The Japanese were even asking how come this sound has caught on internationally. So obviously the music has come a very long way.

'Again, a couple of delegates from Africa found that if they were to drop the rhythm of their own music, they were listening to reggae – which was extremely exciting to find out that maybe this is where the roots of the music came from, from Africa. People from Zimbabwe, Kenya, Nigeria... this is what they were all saying. To slow down their rhythm they found that they were listening back to reggae.

'It made me realise that we haven't even started to sell reggae yet. We'll need the help of big companies, obviously. There is no one in Jamaica who has the finance to really market and distribute the music internationally. But what it means, presumably, is that the big companies who take reggae must realise that it takes time, it's not an overnight big boom; they have got to work at it like any other music. It has got to be worked.' – Neville Lee

Like Harry J, Neville Lee is strongly committed to promoting reggae music internationally. But he is also acutely aware of the problems that invariably arise when the big European-American companies get involved. 'Whilst they are signing,' he points out, 'they are expecting so much that when it doesn't materialise they themselves get frustrated and tend to by-pass the artist. When an artist sells 100-200,000, to them it's still a breaking point. They are not prepared to wait. So in the meantime we in Jamaica continue the best way we can. Although since Bob Marley's death, we have noticed a lot more interest being placed from overseas, and even from our own Caribbean territories where reggae was possibly frowned upon. Bob Marley's death has brought forward some sort of knowledge that this man must have had something to have obtained such a big funeral and big press coverage, and this started people looking into the music.'

Neville Lee's company, Sonic Sound, is essentially a distribution outfit and includes a pressing plant, where the discs are actually manufactured. They are largely orientated towards local artists and producers, offering them both distribution and promotional facilities, and outlets throughout the Caribbean, to the USA, Canada, Britain and some parts of Africa. In contrast to his brother, the notable Byron Lee, whose company controls 80% of the foreign

Overleaf – Robbie Shakespeare and Neville Lee discuss a record deal.

labels distributed in Jamaica (e.g. Polydor, CBS), Neville Lee's operations have 70% of the local labels. But Sonic Sound is still interested in developing its foreign markets and in handling foreign labels in Jamaica as well. 'We already represent foreign labels like EMI, Capital and A&M,' says Lee, 'we have possibly the second best group of foreign labels here. But what we have found in the company is that our first commitment is once again to our own local music.'

In terms of promoting local talent, Sonic Sound adopt a fairly conventional approach, which they say involves breaking the artists first in Jamaica, then re-publicising them in (say) England so that when they and their producers arrive, they are already known and can get a good deal from one of the big companies there. Again, the emphasis on 'the big companies' makes its mark.

In many respects, distribution offers the vital key to expansion into the wider market. Here, the art form (reggae music) is dispersed from a central source, in disc form and not in the shape of local talent as such. Whilst there is no real danger of depleting the pool of talent that already exists in Jamaica, there nevertheless is an uneasy feeling among many people when the 'defection' of some well-known artist to a big Euro-American company is announced. It is thought to represent a loss of some kind, though it is very often difficult to explain. This underlying tension between 'the roots' and commerce is ever present in the Jamaican music business today.

Neville Lee thinks that there is a great deal of untapped potential even within the so-called marginal 'ethnic' markets of the world: 'If we remember that in the UK alone, I think there might be an ethnic market of about 1.8 million Blacks. In possibly the USA there might be doubled that, maybe 3 million. The Caribbean consists of 4½ million people who are already exposed to this music. You are talking about a reasonably good market, which is all ethnic people. It's not crossing over to the whites. Again, reggae has done extremely well in Europe, and the African continent is waiting for the right time for us to export, Yes, the future looks exceptionally good.'

However, Neville Lee does add the important factor of the Jamaican economy, which he feels will ultimately determine the direction that the music business will go. The Jamaican Prime Minister, Mr Edward Seaga, himself an active promotor of Jamaican popular music during the Ska days, reinforces Lee's argument:

'Well I think that the improved economic conditions which we expect, and on which we have already begun to make the turn-around, a definite turn-around, will be good for the artists in various forms of art including folk music and the popular music people – because people can more turn their attention to the field of arts when conditions are more conducive. And the creative artist will have a better market within which to create their products; and in addition to that, of course, the conditions and climate will be the kind in which people can concentrate on enjoying music.

'So the entire atmosphere and prospects are much more healthy over the next several years, than they were over the last several years. How the music will turn one doesn't know – that's in the mind of the artists who are now creating the next stage. One never knew how it was going to turn in the past. What I can say is that we have proven that for a very small country, we have some of the most creative artists in popular music.'

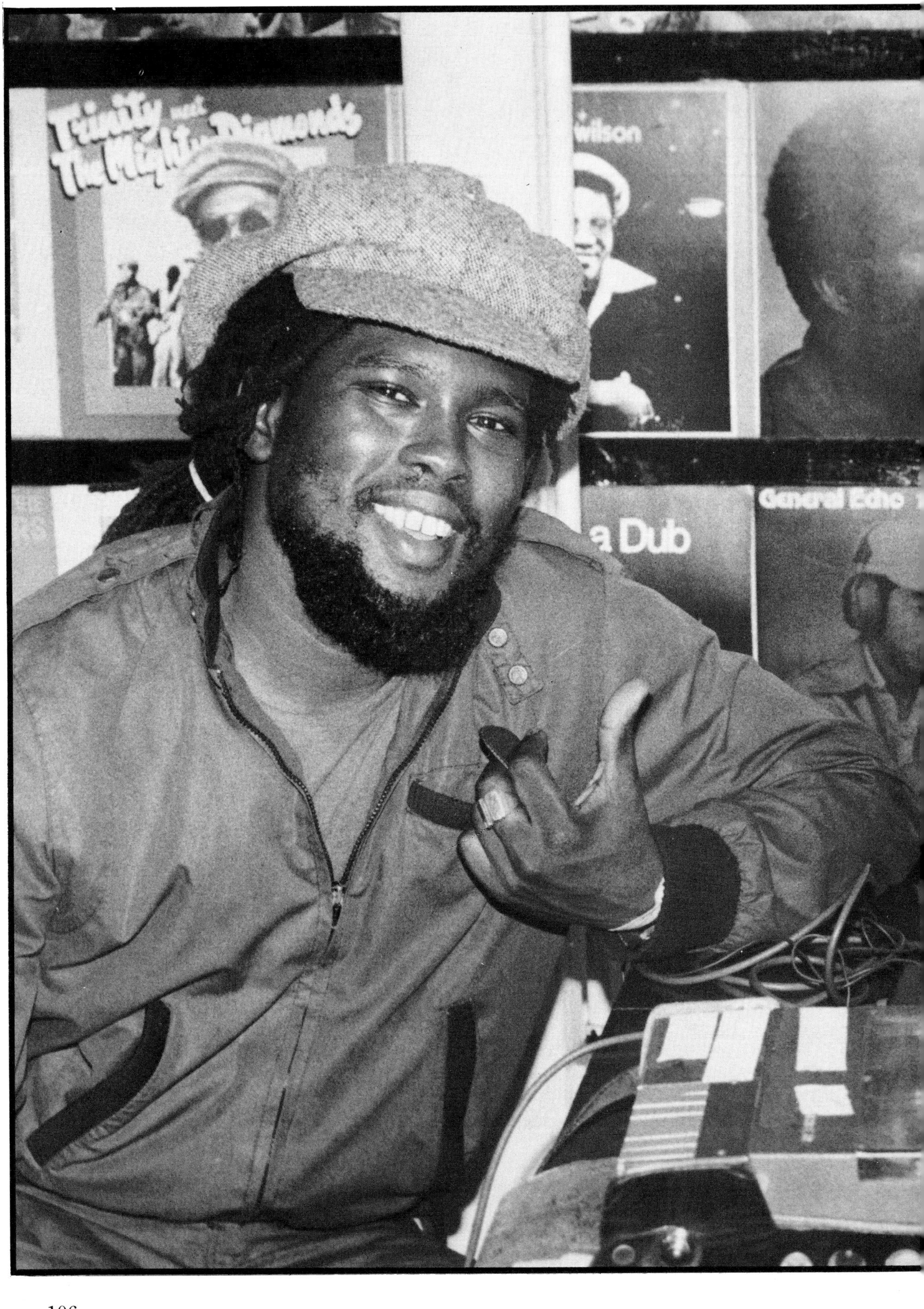
Trinity meet The Mighty Diamonds
wilson
a Dub
General Echo

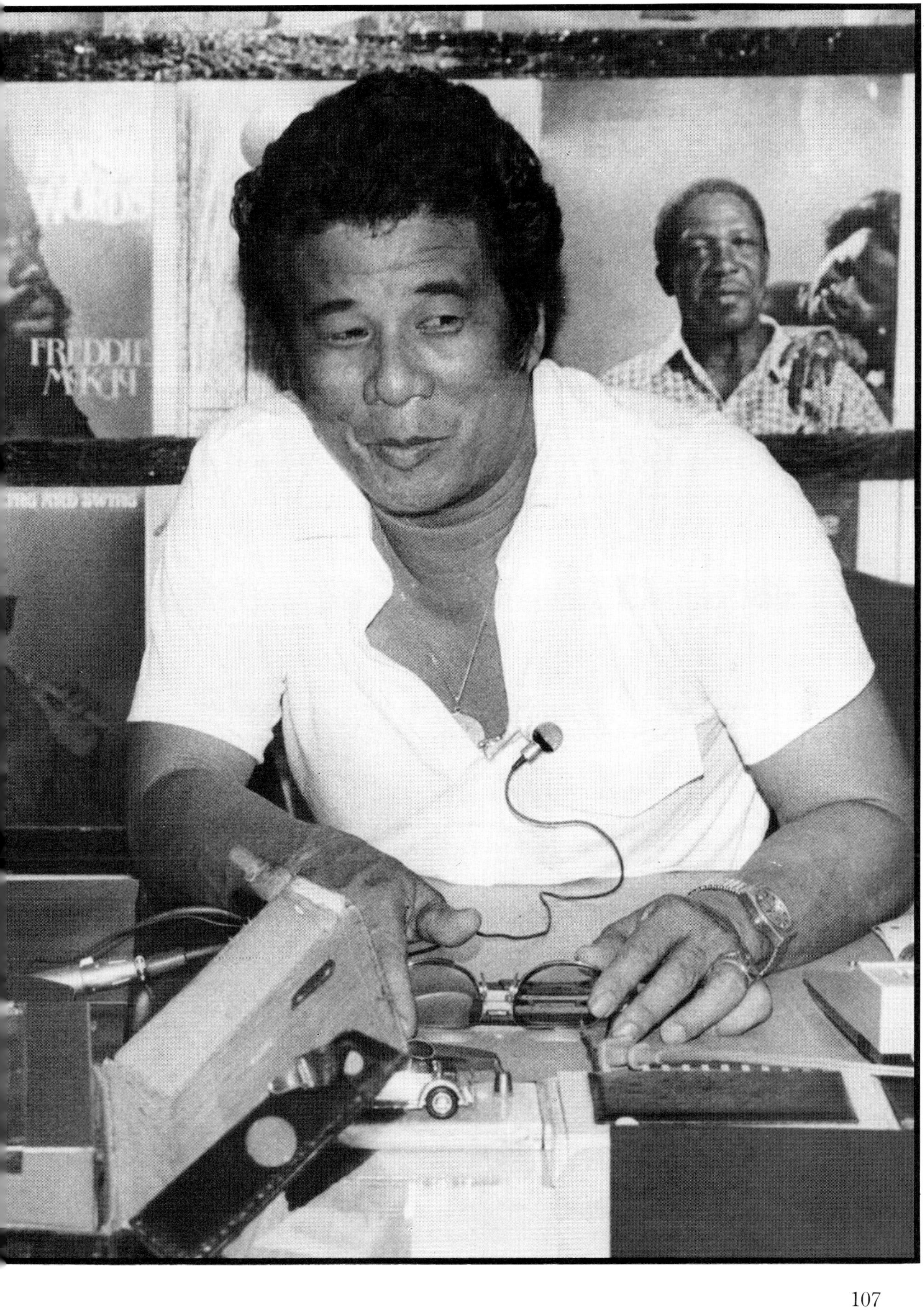

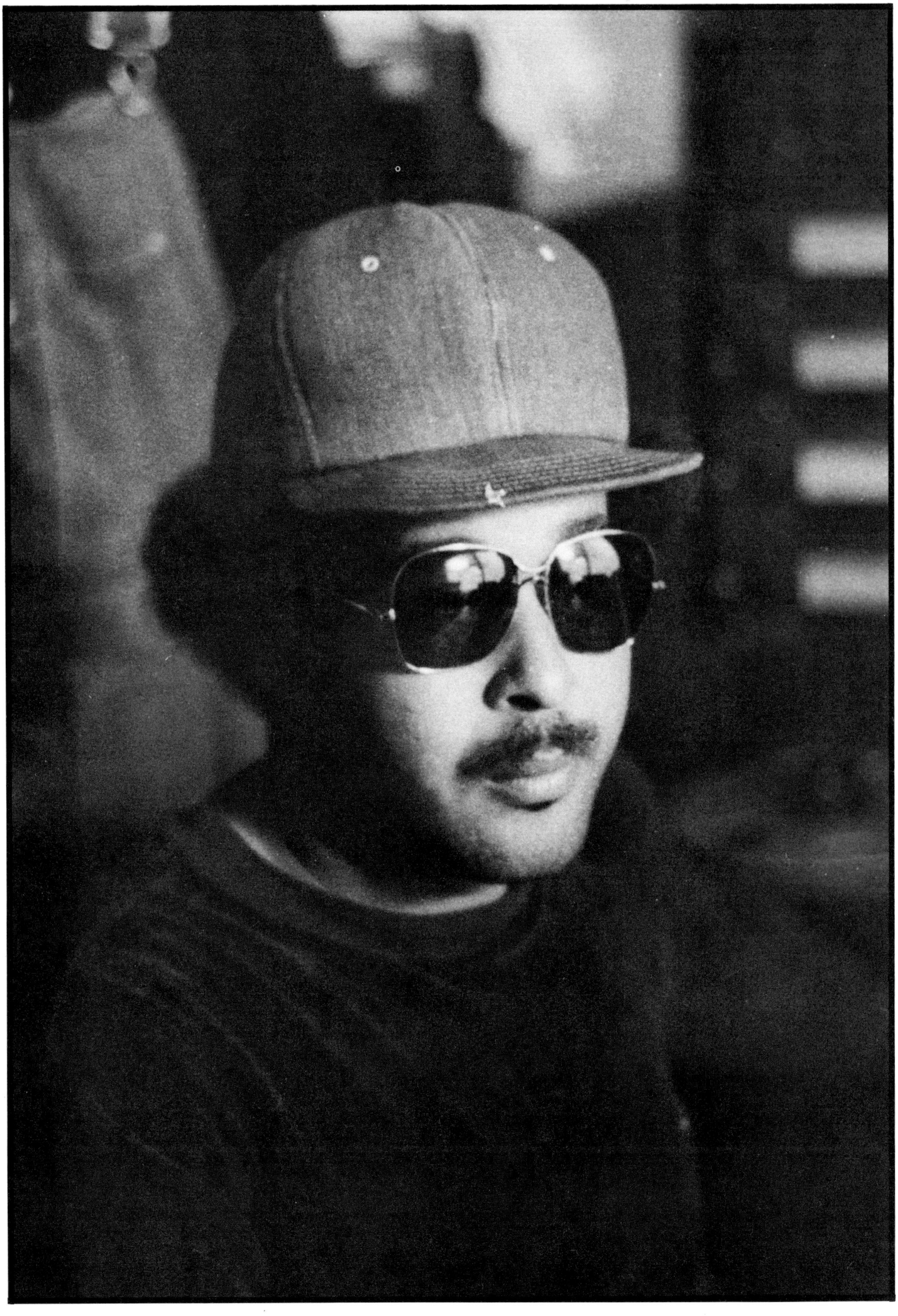

Prince Jammy sitting at his mixing desk at King Tubby's studio.

Reggae music is uniquely Jamaican in character, and this is what has made it work on the minds of both local an international audiences. It is also what has made the music commercially viable: the music is unique in an exciting way. At the same time, however, the power of the music has to be seen in relation to two dimensions – namely, the lyrics (message) and the beat (form). Pamela O'Gorman suggests that there is a kind of tension between these two elements in the music: politically evocative lyrics on the one hand, and an absorbing beat on the other. In other words, the message is very often taken over by the seductive dance rhythm of the music.

'I think one of the problems,' states Ms O'Gorman, 'is that the lyrics of the songs are not listened to carefully enough. In fact, Bob Marley himself at one time complained that people didn't *listen* to his songs – he said 'don't just move to the music, listen to what I'm saying'. I think that goes for a lot of reggae artists who obviously are trying to get across a message, trying to say something to the rest of the population – and very often in inflammatory terms, in very direct terms. Whether these messages succeed in getting through entirely or not, I don't know. Because, of course, the overriding element in reggae is the beat. Even in the way the music is produced, that is, in having a heavy beat that comes up and almost obliterates the voice line. You find that because the music is balanced in this particular way, people will just start to move to the beat; they will feel this bass in their chest; and very often a lot of sense of the words will be lost.'

The problem that Pamela O'Gorman raises is highlighted especially in the way that reggae music is often promoted abroad – where it is first and foremost an entertainment medium which is locked into a commercial structure. In this context, we would also have to consider how 'pop music' generally functions in this society, and the extent to which reggae music gets absorbed into that set of values. But the fact remains, it is the musicians themselves who create the music. And though they are completely at the mercy of the producers and distributors, who greatly influence the circulation of their songs, they nevertheless continue to write that has political significance.

'I think that if the musicians didn't feel that they had that power to influence things through their music,' concludes Pamela O'Gorman, 'they wouldn't bother to compose the songs in the first place. Because there can be no doubt that reggae music in Jamaica has done a tremendous amount to make people aware of the suffering of the people in the ghetto, the feeling of white oppression of the Black man, the feeling of Black pride, the messages of Marcus Garvey particularly, and Rastafari – all these things have really embedded themselves in the consciousness of the population through reggae.'

The broader economic arguments and the moves to establish reggae music in 'its rightful place in the world of popular music', therefore, have to be seen in close relation to the social *and* political function that reggae music continues to have in Jamaican society today.

St. John surrounded by Black Kush.

GHETTO RIDDIMS

"Early on your duties:" Young man sings struggling music for Jack Ruby (left)

'Me is the man who don't think in terms of politics from the level of the P.N.P. or the J.L.P., because I figure more or less that politics play a lot of games with poor people's lives. You dig. I am dealing with the music of reality, like telling you what happen over there, why John is killing Tom, and a lot of these things is because of political talk within the people. From I was a kid till now I still hear the man them singing about "Island in the sun" and it more look like "Island with a gun" now, you see. And the people are still singing that. They're not really giving privilege to these youths but to ah one who wants to sound like Teddy Pendergrass or wants to sound like Elvis Presley. And you have true people who create music which I think we should publicise ... I think we need to produce and promote more of our own production.' – Jack Ruby

Jack Ruby, the legendary sound system operator and producer, is passionate about the harsh realities of everyday life in Jamaican society, and he is an ardent promoter of the music that comes out of that experience – 'roots' reggae. He was the original producer of the great Burning Spear, whose music rekindled the flame of Marcus Garvey. It is significant, indeed, that Marcus Garvey, Burning Spear, Bob Marley and Jack Ruby all came from the same area, St. Anne's Bay near Maroon Town – and they all continued the tradition of struggle which began with the Maroon warrior.

Today, Jack Ruby holds auditions in his backyard, as young musicians come from miles around to sing the kind of songs he likes to hear. They are the young hopefuls – many of them will go on to make records, some will become stars. During the auditions, everyone gets involved in discussions about the social and political conditions which affect their lives. One of the musicians describes what inspired his song, 'Tribulation':

'Well, I've seen a lot of tribulation among the people. It's I who Jah give the message to bring it out into the people. You know, my people around me, and even to the four ends of the earth. Because Jah really sends a messenger each time to speak to His people.'

Jack Ruby, among others, nevertheless believes that the trend is moving more towards commercialisation, despite efforts by a number of leading producers to retain the 'roots' qualities in the music that they produce. At the same time, however, it is the people who really create the music; and if the people themselves are under increasing pressure from above, this will come across in the music that they create. Reggae music is still the main vehicle for unity in the ghetto areas. It invokes a body of themes and images around which participants can relate. This seems to be one of the significant things about Jack Ruby's backyard auditions – it is an experience which activates a sense of communality, where groups of people can assess daily the lesser-known but vibrant music that is being created by the younger generation today.

But because of its importance to the people, music has been one of the cultural areas that the status quo has actively co-opted and used as a form of social control, against the very people who created the music in the first place. 'The politicians have to use the music,' states Jack Ruby, 'because God says music alone shall live. Politics is a folly. The music controls the mind of people. So at all times, whenever the strong get weak – and right now on earth, not just Jamaica, even the strong get weak at times – and when the strong get weak they turn to the weak for assistance. So the music, what the people sing, it

Tribulation Man sings of "Tribulation" for Jack Ruby, accompanied by Mickey Simpson on guitar. (He was found that same day singing by a riverside.)

elevates the people more than what the politicians tell them – because it's pure friction what the politician and preacher tell Black people; and the people get so sick of that, that with the music they will swing and rock and not listen to what the brother says, and just get into the music. An individual politician might use an individual record which is a hit song in the people's mind, so the people sing along to that, so immediately it's like they get indoctrinated because the music leads people, y'know.

'Even the sound system, you're surprised to see how many hundreds of people just come out and can't pay to come in and dance. But they don't leave till daylight because its the only comfort they have, it's the only meditation within the mind, because them have so much problem that the music takes away the problem for a little while. Bob Marley sing some tunes that they used in the election he cool down the fight because the youth got crazy.

'A man just fires his gun on a brother for nothing. The political people give them the gun to get the power by scaring certain people or to destroy certain communities. That is how it works, from either side. Each gunman will defeat the other side of the people, there is always a tug-of-war with the people. But when it reaches a time that election is done, or enough money is not functioning, the same youth who got the gun to fire for election, go and fire it on a man and takes away the few dollars he earns. It's an American gun, yes man, M 16 – what they used in Vietnam to kill enough Chinamen, they pass on to kill up the Black man. You see the argument that arises here.

'Let's bring the argument back to the music. If you listen to half of the D.J.'s, you hear them hackling about the "16 connection". Even the D.J.'s pick that up. If it was a cooler runnings and that never happened, they would talk about something else...' 'It's like them see too much movie now,' a youth interjects. 'Your cameraman

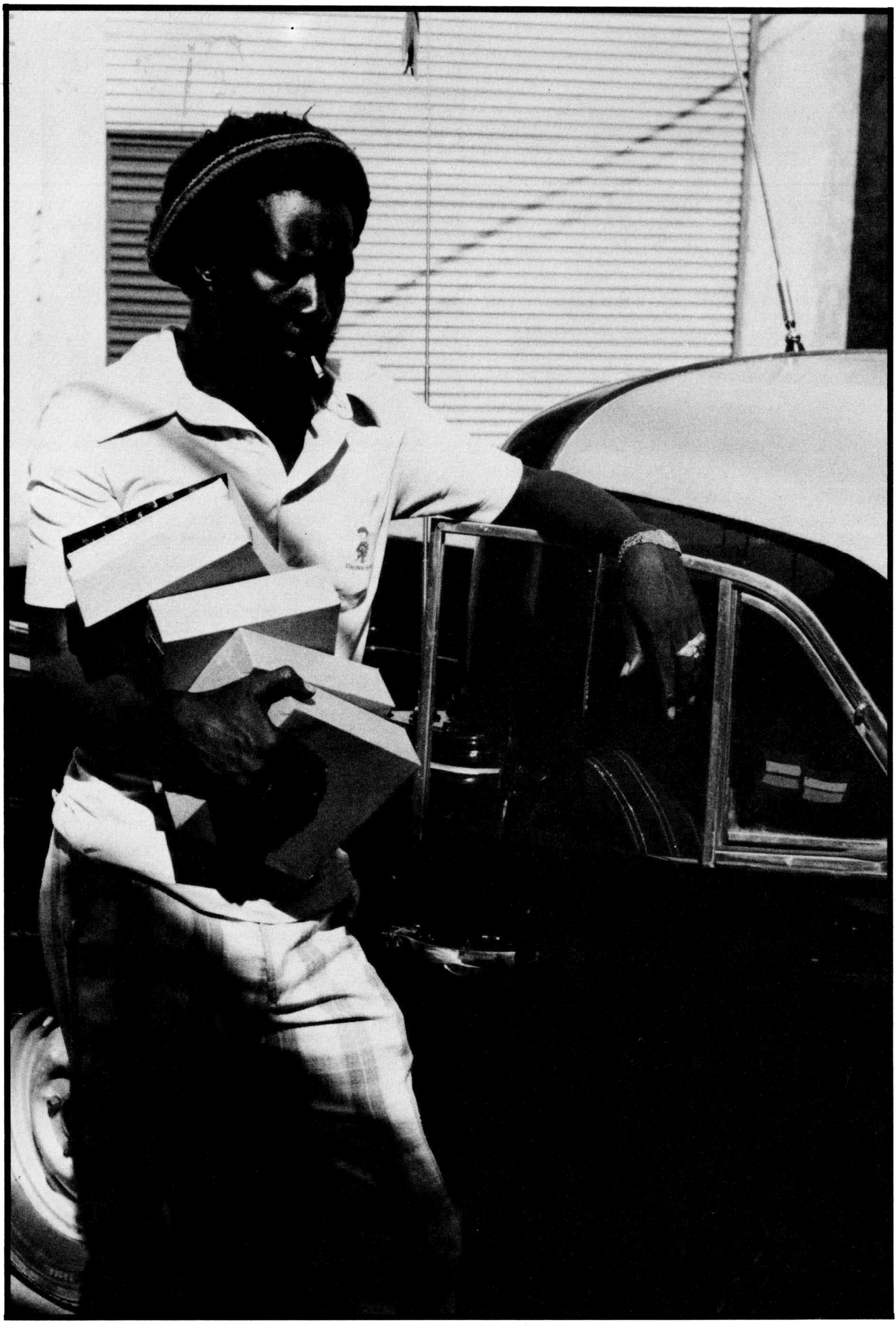

Opposite – **Charlie Ace buys records for his record shack. Left- Charlie Ace's record shack stands at the corner of parade playing music for the ghetto people.**

Overleaf – **Big Youth tells Pepe Judah that this sensimilia field goes on for miles and miles.**

couldn't stand up between those guys if they wanted to film this,' continues Jack Ruby, It's too hot. The cameraman would fling away his camera and run. (Laughter) You wonder how man get so many shots, shots bark from dust till dawn. You hear all the D.J.'s telling you, BLAP! BLAP! BLAP!...' Asked what kind of gun it is, a Youth replies, 'I don't know. They put it on a stand and push it on a wheel barrow – POP! POP! POP!...'

'But right now it looks a bit cooler than before the election [of 1980],' concludes Jack Ruby, 'And I hope it continues, because too much people dead. Too much youth dead.'

'Why don't I get a shop? Right now I find it this way much better, you know. I and I owner where I do I things. Every other man is shop, shop, shop. Well for I-self, if money come I just mobile, mobile, mobile. I and I play music everyday daily from eight right on through, because in a way this is how I make my two. And I enjoy it. People from all over the world come and hear: some buy, some just rock. Them just get in the groove because as you know, it's a get-together sound, reggae music.' – Charlie Ace

Charlie Ace operates a mobile record 'shop', bringing reggae music records to the back streets of Kingston. He is like a latter-day 'buru-man', loved and respected by the community.

'Right here I can get to move around in the ghetto, because it's the ghetto people who really support this thing. Reggae music from way back for years, you know, because reggae music is one of them stones that was refused by the builders. But like it is said, the stone that the builders refused shall be the head corner stone; and brother I tell you, I enjoy playing music right now in the ghetto and for all these years it's the poor people them support it. As soon as a guy get big, him will want to just move up town, you dig. So right now it's just I and I in the ghetto. A-rock the people daily. Sometimes when they broke and feel downhearted the music keep them going... It is Jah, you know, who give I the idea.

'To play music to poor Black people? Yes man, because I meet youth and youth on yah daily, and down here and I and I suffering youth reason, and I can show them where I'm coming from – same place, in the ghetto. And show them that they can try a thing like I, instead of pure M16 and shooting down brethren. One Love.'

'Politics is a fantasy.' – Black Kush

Four hundred years of slavery and oppression – and Jamaica's dread poets, philosophers, musicians and warriors continue to make their voices heard and their presence felt. They have built even mightier towers on the foundations laid by their ancestors, the Maroons. A new generation of reggae artists has emerged out of the ghetto, like Black Kush, armed with the same passion as their ancestors and even greater, sharper awareness of the workings of the Babylonian ideology and technology. And their target is global.

'Reggae's the King's music, music which speaks out against oppression and injustice and cries for equality. Right now South Africa is the last stronghold of the great white empire and Rastafari says by 1983 it must be free; and before one of his words fail heaven and earth shall move because Russia and America must worry if South Africa is not free, you understand. So you see we must play the King's music

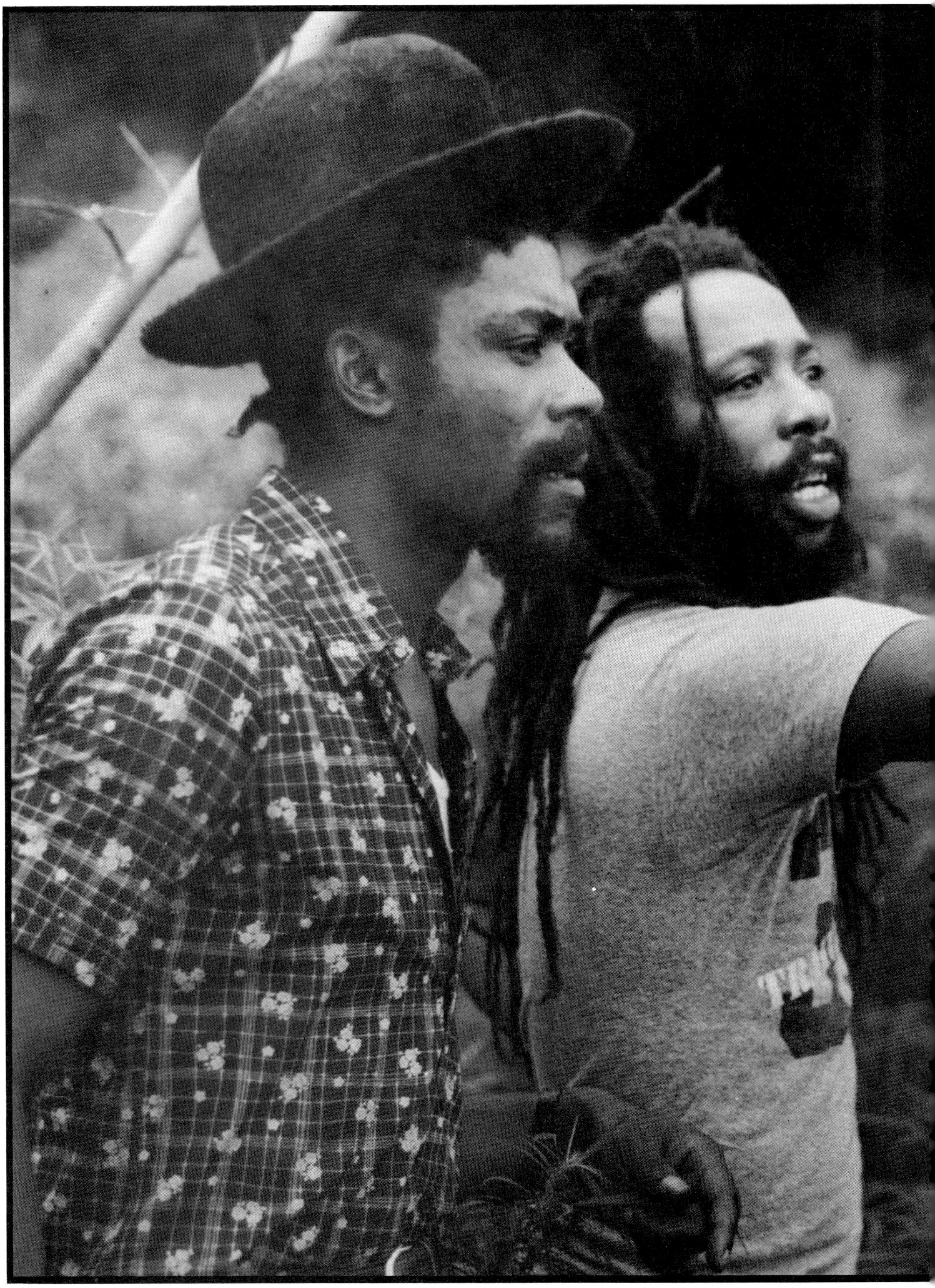

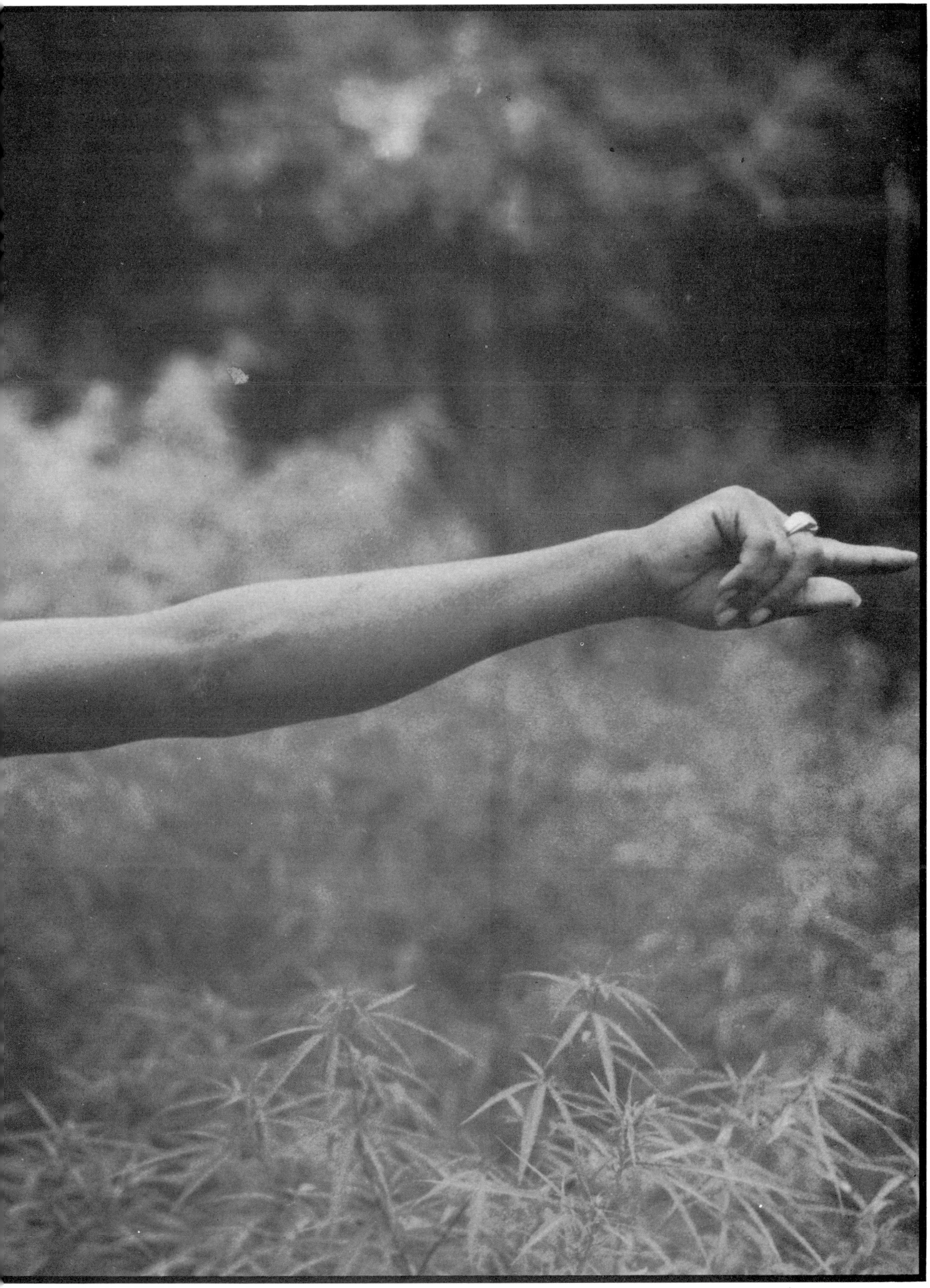

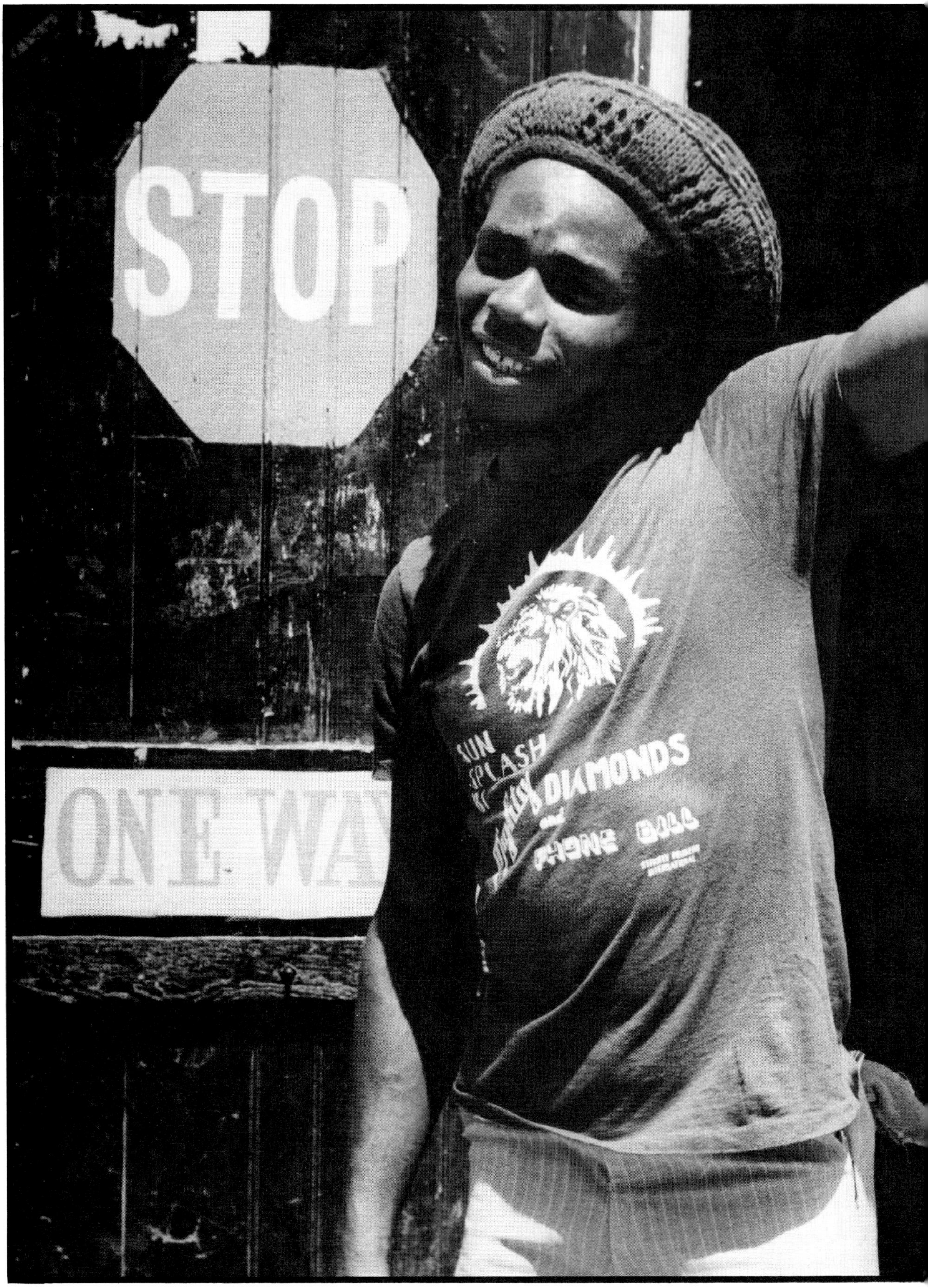
STOP
ONE WA
SUN
SPLASH
DIAMONDS

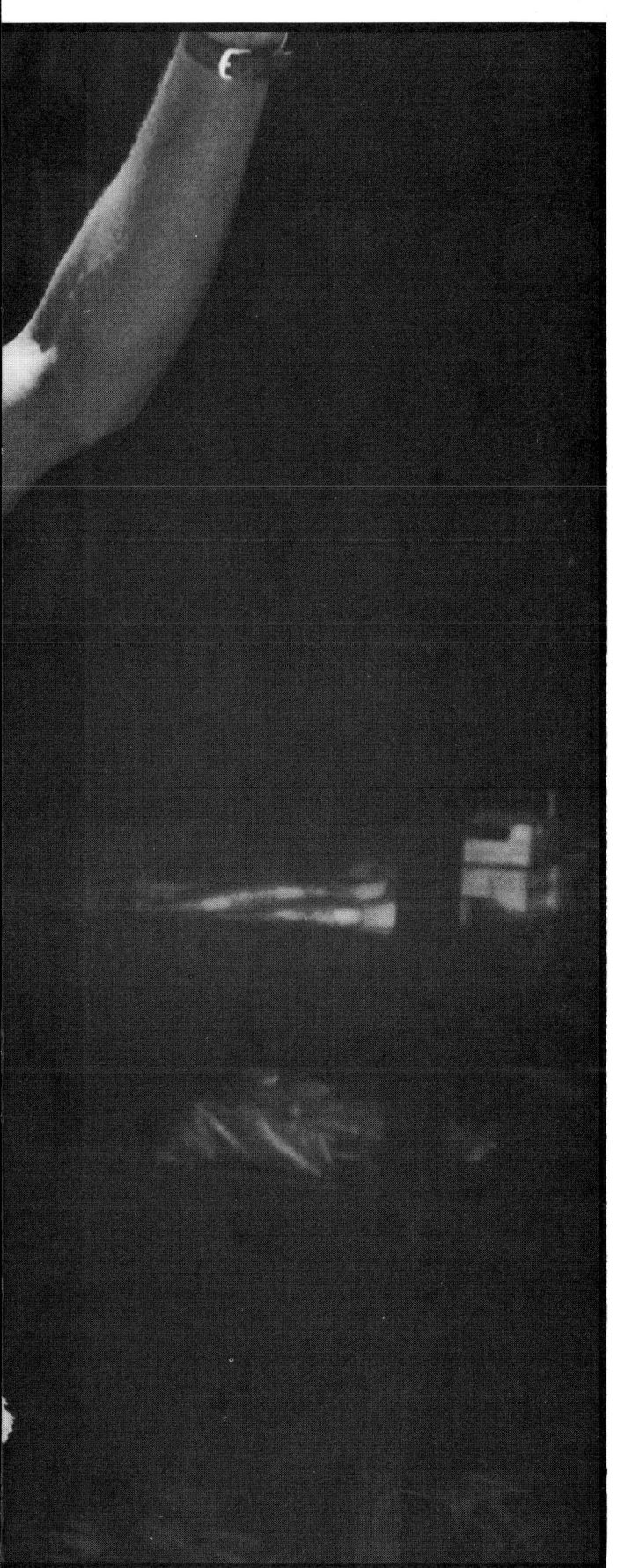

The brilliant Tabby, lead singer of the Mighty Diamonds.

because we're coming in righteousness. And now we're crying out that we want our flag to be raised in peace and truth – which is the Red, Green and Gold flag – without fear or favour or apology. Rastafari Selassie-I and that is our worst trouble today. You see there are those who are marching onto war, making MX bombs and SS-20 bombs and more – pure weapons of destruction. Everything they build is destruction.

'Instruments of cruelty and war, and marching in the name of Jesus Christ. I and I are the righteous children, we are the seeds and the servants of His Majesty. We listen to the voice from the throne and we're marching with our guitars and our harps and our string instruments. You understand? We're going head on to meet the devil with his guns, you understand, because we don't fear.

'Reggae music, created from the plantation – just like your heart beat sound when you hear the slave master ah come. The sound of Reggae Music, the heart beat sound in reggae music that fear when you see the slave master you know. If you sing upon the plantation you have to be quiet, but reggae music is from them. Long I-Wa jazz music, jazz music. Reggae music. The music that make us feel happy. Me never need to go to school and study Beethoven or Bach, Stravinsky or anyone like that to learn notes. This music come from the heart, it's a genetic transmission, a higher science. Selassie-I. Rastafari Selassie-I don't look backward, for there's a kingdom, there's a land that has been promised and we're sure of it, God must come. By 1990 we see our victory.

'Listen man, if this was all the living down yah so, life is miserable, Yeah man. If this is all the living, life would be so miserable ah-no so Jah make it feh go. I and I ah go live, I and I ah go irie life – which is why we want repatriation. It's a

Right – **Sly Dunbar** (in white hat) at rehearsals. Facing top – **Leggo Beast** prepares to fill the chillum. Facing bottom – **Dillinger** sitting on his Honda at Idlers Rest.

must. Life is miserable. I couldn't so Jah make it feh go.

'Yes, I and I give thanks to the great Bob Marley that passed away. Yes, he gone far up and left his etchings that I and I could fulfill it. It's like Bob opened the gate and gone to set up in a higher place. I and I must just continue with the works.'

'My philosophy,' states the great Saint John, manager and mentor of Black Kush, 'is like this: the army and police and all those people, instead of giving them guns, they should give them hammer and saw to build houses for poor people. But you see, the rich want to maintain all the resources in the earth. Instead of giving them guns, all reason and thing, give them hammer and saw to build houses for poor people. People would be less violent and thing. They wouldn't have to label people as terrorists and all that, and categorise I-man. But who is them to define I and I. Who are they to define I and I reality?

'His majesty has said the word and the word is. Until that philosophy which holds one race superior and another inferior is finally discredited and finally abandoned, them know the rest of it still, everywhere is war. Bob Marley sing it, SEEN. Reggae addresses a social issue in the same sense as did the blues in the U.S.A. It was a cry against a particular condition, you see. Black man in the United States during the evolution of the blues was crying out "Oh!" They were longing for their woman, mainly because they were isolated. Those who took us away in chains and made us sit by the banks of the rivers of Babylon, they wanted us to wear white things on our lips, gloves, and tap dance like a coon. But we didn't want to do that. We wanted to cry the music for the King of Kings, to let the world know that the condition that we were living in wasn't pleasing, wasn't acceptable, you see.

'Now through the media, which is controlled by the forces of evil at this particular time, they only advocate or exhibit things that are likened to them, that can benefit them, and they don't show the real picture. For example, in Jamaica now, they show you about tourism and all that stuff; but they won't show the conditions that exist in the ghetto. When they're running a documentary on tourism, they're trying to let people live a life of illusion, an illusionary life, when there is a more tangent reality that we must face and accept, which is documented in the Bible.

'You see in the Bible, in Revelation, Rastafari fight against the great whore Mother Babylon, who had all the delicacies in the world – meaning she had colour T.V. and carpet, refrigerator, etc., while we down here shuffling to buy a piece of ice for twenty-five cents and can't get it, and drinking pipe water, SEEN. We have it hard, that's who Rastafari fight – the great Whore and the Beast who deceive the nation, meaning anyone who go and continually lie about the Jesus Christ in the sky going to come and redeem the earth – which is a myth! *SEEN.*'

121

The legendary Bob Marley, playing his guitar before his last concert at Crystal Palace, 1980.

"2000 years of black history could not be wiped out so easily."

TWENTY ALBUMS / TWENTY SINGLES

Noel Hawks & Chris Lane

The following records are not placed in any order of merit because, in their own way, they are all brilliant – classics if you like. What they hopefully do is give some indication of all the important different styles, artists and producers in the development of electric Jamaican music. Further investigation of anyone mentioned below will definitely prove worthwhile.

Noel Hawks' L.P.s

Ska Authentic – **The Skatalites** – Studio One
Prod: C.S. Dodd

One has to overcome the usual prejudices about ska before settling into an appreciation, as its frantic pace and generally indecipherable vocals can be off-putting. The seeds of all that was to follow are here as the music transcends its R & B influences and begins to take on a life and vitality all of its own.

Version Galore – **U Roy** – Treasure Isle
Prod: Duke Reid

It's never been the same since Roy woke the town and told the people in the early 70's. Even though live D.J.'s or toasters were nothing new and King Stitt had already made his mark as a recording artist U Roy changed everything with his jive talking, nonsense rhyming 100m.p.h. delivery. Whooping, hollering, seeming to argue and agree with Treasure Isle's greatest rocksteady vocals, this still sounds just as exciting today as it did then. Every track is a sheer joy and the key word is FUN.

Love Me Forever – **Carlton & His Shoes** – Studio One
Prod: C. S. Dodd

There's not a lot besides love songs here but Carlton Manning is quite simply the best singer to ever come out of Jamaica. Over the last fifteen years, backed either by his brothers Donald & Lynford, various Studio One session men or even double and treble tracking himself he has produced some of the finest reggae and rocksteady close harmony music to ever grace vinyl. Difficult to describe as a greatest hits collection, as he hasn't enjoyed a great deal of commercial success during his long career, the set is nevertheless essential to an understanding of the music outside of the roots/rasta spectrum.

Blackheart Man – **Bunny Wailer** – Solomonic
Prod: Bunny Wailer

It's sad that in the years after his first solo outing Bunny's following has grown and grown while the quality of his music (with a few notable exceptions) has steadily declined. Intense, personal, spiritual and immaculately executed with the aid of the top Kingston session musicians there's few better testaments to the Rastafarian influence on reggae music.

The Heptones – **The Heptones** – Studio One
On Top – **The Heptones** – Studio One
Prod: C. S. Dodd

I know it's cheating but I'm making no apologies or excuses. Three-part close harmonies were the mainstay of rocksteady and reggae and the Heptones were the undisputed leaders in the field. They set the standards on their first two L.P.'s for the others to measure their contributions by. Timeless music.

African Herbsman – **Bob Marley & The Wailers** – Trojan Trls 62 (U.K.)
Prod: Lee Perry & Bob Marley

Island Records made the Wailers international reputation but to find out what attracted their interest originally it's necessary to check this record in particular and all of their earlier output. Trojan records put this together in this country (it was never released in Jamaica) and it contains striking examples of the best Upsetter material and some early Tuff Gong self-productions. Crucial.

I'm Flash Forward – **Cedric I'm Brooks** – Studio One
Prod: C. S. Dodd

Equally essential are Jackie Mittoo's Macka Fat and Roland Alphonso's Best Of & King Of Sax. All feature top class musicians producing top class music over top class rhythms. The bias towards Coxsone Dodd's Studio One organisation is completely intentional by the way.

King Tubby Meets The Rockers Uptown – **Augustus Pablo** – Yard
Prod: Augustus Pablo

The most interesting thing about Pablo's productions has always been when King Tubby took over the controls and here we have a collection of these B-sides which serve to define dub music.

Pirate's Choice – **Various Artists** – Studio One
Prod: C. S. Dodd

Left to his own devices it's unlikely that Mr Dodd would have put out a compilation as good as this, after all two good tracks will sell an L.P., but the record pirates forced his hand when they released the bootleg "Best of Studio One Vol. Four". The pirates' choice was impeccable, covering the vast range and scope of 70's Studio One output, but Coxsone's own issue of the compilation is worth owning for the cover alone.

Live Loving – **Sugar Minott** – Studio One
Prod: C. S. Dodd

Sugar's personality and talent are definite bright hopes for the future. His first L.P. was like a ray of light in the late 70's and he's already kept and improved on the promise of his early work. Startling originality is not what he's all about but his adoptions and adaptations of existing idioms are more than worth following up.

SINGLES:

On the Beach – **Owen Grey** – Coxsone
Prod: C. S. Dodd

Originally intended as nothing more than a replica of R & B extolling the virtues of Coxsone's Sound System, Owen Grey's advertisement is interesting for it's loping beat but essential for it's name dropping: "I was dancing to the music of Sir Coxsone the Downbeat on the beach…".

54-56 That's My Number – **The Maytals** – Beverley's
Prod: Lesley Kong

The popularity of Lesley Kong and the Maytals has slipped since the early 70's but this 1968 recording shows them at the height of their powers. Perhaps Kong wasn't always particularly innovative but his chugging rocksteady backing provided the perfect foil for the Maytals hoarse vocals.

Harbour Shark – **Pipe & The Pipers** – Tuff Gong
Prod: Alan Cole

To avoid any confusion with the Wailers the Wailing Souls became Pipe & The Pipers when they recorded for the Wailers Tuff Gong label. Winston Matthews has never bettered the lyrics or the arrangement and to hear him in this context is to hear what an original and inventive talent he possesses.

Sky Juice/Not Long Ago – **Big Youth** – Augustus Buchanan
Prod: Big Youth

A stylistic and lyrical innovator Big Youth set the standard for D.J.'s to actually say something rather than simply urge on dancers. Sky Juice is a frozen drink sold from carts in downtown Kingston but it becomes a vehicle for Big Youth's guided tour of the "Sufferers style in the ghetto" life.

In Their Own Way – **Dennis Brown** – African Museum
Prod: Gregory Isaacs

A cutting rhythm, incisive lyric and Dennis' heartfelt vocal add up to one of the finest examples of sufferers' music ever made.

One One Cocoa Full Basket – **Gregory Isaacs** – Dwyer
Prod: Glen Brown

Superstar Mr Isaacs has seldom looked back and his popularity just goes from strength to strength. One of the earliest and best examples of his unique singing style and philosophy is this subtle, controlled slice of dynamism.

Best Dressed Chicken – **Dr. Alimantado** – Capo
Prod: Dr. Alimantado

Coming from the same D.J. School as Big Youth and leaning heavily on Lee Perry's production talents the ital surgeon is the only eccentric to make the list – and there were more than enough to choose from. The track is so outrageous that it had to be included but sadly he's never bettered it.

Daughters of Zion – **Prince Lincoln** – Studio One
Prod: C.S. Dodd

A soaring voice and finely honed thoughtful songs are Prince Lincoln Thompson's trademarks and he's hopefully back on the right track after a misguided attempt at pop stardom, for he has the ability to break big on his own terms. His self-productions are always interesting but a sympathetic Studio One backing is all that's required here.

Right Time – **Mighty Diamonds** – Well Charge
Prod: Jo Jo Hookim

The Diamonds happened to be in the right place at the right time (Channel One Studios in 1975) and their sound was to captivate reggae listeners for a long time to come. Always followers rather than leaders their relaxed yet urgent prophesying borrowed from a number of sources but came together beautifully on a number of classic sides.

Love Thy Neighbour – **Vivian Jackson** – Deffenders
Prod: Aston Barrett

Self-styled "Jesus Dread" Vivian Jackson or Yabby You has always been a cut above the rasta sermonising school. In fact, in many ways, he's been largely responsible for it but many of the others lacked his warmth and reality. It's important to remember that he means every word, yet to so many others it was a way of achieving fame and money neither of which he's seen too much of.

Chris Lane's L.P.s

Bob Andy's Songbook – **Bob Andy** – Studio One
Prod: C. S. Dodd

This brilliant anthology of Bob's classic rock-steady hits showcases his progressive writing style, as well as highlighting some of Jackie Mittoo's best, and most-copied rhythm arrangements.

Early Days – **Slim Smith** – Total Sounds
Prod: Bunny Lee

The late Slim Smith was rock-steady's finest singer, in the Curtis Mayfield mould but with an edge to his voice that sometimes verged on hysteria.

Ska-Boo-Da-Ba – **Skatalites** – Wirl
Prod: Phillip Yap

Another of Jamaica's late, great musical heroes, Don Drummond was *the* jazz/ska trombonist, and this mainly instrumental album features him on some of his moodiest performances, including the timeless "Confucious".

Dub Store Special – Coxsone
Prod: C. S. Dodd

The most varied of the Studio One's dub L.P.'s with some of the tracks featuring Cedric Brooks on tenor sax. This and the other early Studio One dub albums (Hi-Fashion, Mellow, Better and Ital) demonstrate engineer Sylvan Morris' ability to get more feel out of dub-mixing two-track rhythms than most engineers can get out of four, eight or sixteen.

This is Augustus Pablo – **Augustus Pablo** – Kaya
Prod: Clive Chin

Augustus Pablo had a profound effect on Jamaican music during the seventies. Firstly because of his "Far East" melodica playing, secondly because of his keyboard work on sessions. This L.P. still remains his best purely instrumental (as opposed to dub) album, most of his best self-productions being on deleted singles.

Marcus Garvey – **Burning Spear** – Fox
Prod: Jack Ruby

The title track re-launched Spear's career in late '74, and he never looked back, although he often re-records his classic Studio One tracks that can be found on the early '70's album "Studio One Presents" and "Rocking Time".

Mr Soul of Jamaica – **Alton Ellis** – Treasure Isle
Prod: Duke Reid

Alton was, and still is, reggae's most soulful singer/songwriter, and this collection of Treasure Isle hits should be enough to convince you of that. If not, then listen to his Studio One albums as well.

Hottest Hits – **V/A** – Treasure Isle
Prod: Duke Reid

A collection of Treasure Isle's all-time classics, which includes tracks by the Paragons, Techniques, Melodians, Sensations and Alton Ellis. Tommy McCook, leader of the Supersonics, was responsible for Treasure Isle's magnificent cool, relaxed sound.

Presenting – **I Roy** – Gussie
Prod: Gussie Clarke

I Roy was always the most intellectual deejay – long words, proper sentences, could probably even read and write. On rhythms like these he couldn't fail, and as usual with deejays, his first L.P. caught him at his best.

Skylarking – **Horace Andy** – Studio One
Prod: C.S. Dodd

Horace Hinds (re-named 'Andy', after Bob, as a tribute to his songwriting) has a fairly strange voice, which after a while can become an obsession. Many Jamaican singers owe their sucess to his influence, including current hit-maker Eek-A-Mouse.

SINGLES:

Satta A Masa Gana – **Abysinnians** – Clinch
Prod: Bernard Collins

Their first record, made at Studio One with the Sound Dimension, took two years to become a hit. Now it's a Rastafarian anthem.

Al Capone – **Prince Buster All Stars** – Prince Buster
Prod: Prince Buster

This ska classic is still being played in pop discos every night, and has probably done more for Jamaican music than any other record.

Joy In The Morning – **Gaylads** – Wirl
Prod: Wirl

A beautiful song written by the Gaylad's own Delano Stewart, complete with perfect rhythm arrangement from guitarist Lynn Taitt & His Jets – an excellent example of non-Studio One/Treasure Isle rock-steady.

Hyprocrites – **Bob Marley & The Wailing Wailers** – Wail'n'Soul'm
Prod: Bob Marley

My favourite Wailer's record, without doubt. From their short-lived (but artistically successful) self-produced period between Studio One and Beverley's.

The Way It Is – **I. Kong** – Top Cat
Prod: Tommy Cowan & Errol Kong

A moody sufferer's lament, which never resorts to any of the usual Rasta cliches.

Dry Up Your Tears – **Bruce Ruffin** – Beverley's
Prod: Leslie Kong

A typical reggae lover's classic from the Beverley's stable, with Ruffin's voice floating over the Dynamites' restrained, but ever-so-tight backing.

Tonight – **Keith & Tex** – Move & Groove
Prod: Derrick Harriott

Keith Rowe and Tex Dixon made only a handful of records for one of Jamaica's most meticulous singer/producers, Derrick Harriott, "Tonight" being the best of a brilliant bunch.

Words of Wisdom – **Light of Saba** – Saba
Prod: Cedric Brooks

A warning to wrong-doers from Michael Rastar & The Light of Saba, a Rastafarian band led by Cedric 'I'm' Brooks. They sound infinitely more sincere than most current dreadlocked 'cultural' bands.

Place Called Africa – **Junior Byles** – Justice League
Prod: Lee Perry

Junior Byles was Scratch's finest discovery, and although many Upsetter records date badly (through Perry's inspired/eccentric production ideas), this one stands the test of time.

You'll Get Your Pay – **Linton Cooper** – Money Disc
Prod: C.S. Dodd

The advantages in having your own studio are not purely financial – musicians on a weekly wage can spend more time on their own ideas and occasionally come up with something as odd as this record. A timeless 'reality' lyric, an exceptionally miserable vocal performance, and possibly reggae's most out-of-tune piano all add up to an unforgettable record.